Mrs Wordsmith®

EPIC WORDS

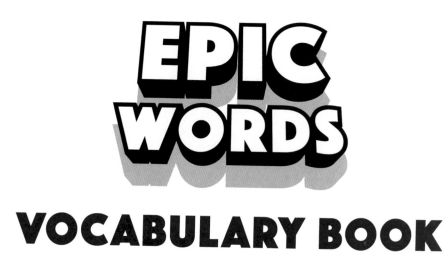

VOCABULARY BOOK

Written and illustrated
by Mrs Wordsmith

MEET THE CHARACTERS

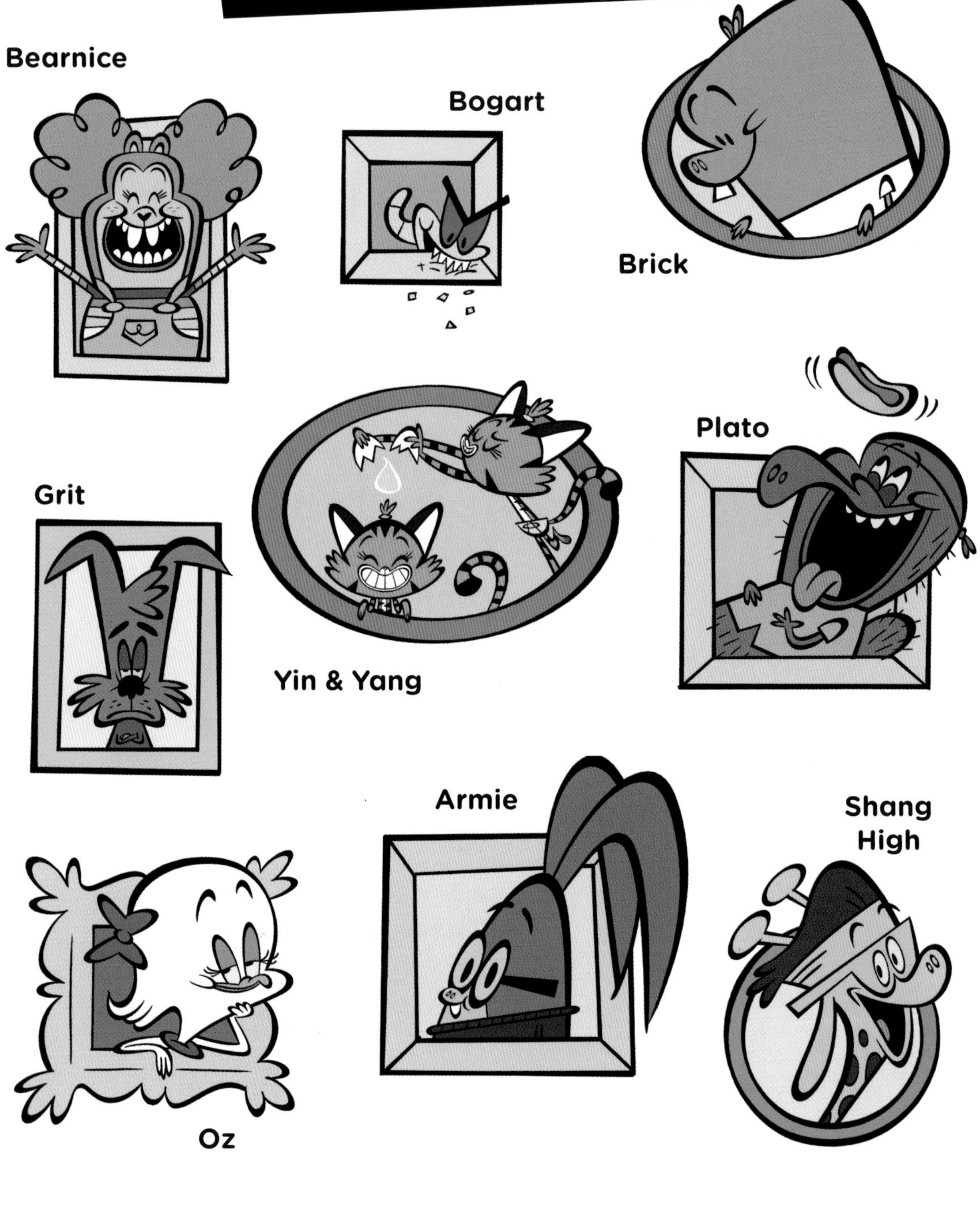

Bearnice
Bogart
Brick
Grit
Yin & Yang
Plato
Armie
Shang High
Oz

CONTENTS

Get to know your vocabulary book 9

WORDS FOR...

Epic me 13
Time 49
Numbers, shapes, and sizes 61
Where and how 77
Technology 89
Learning and creating 111
Everyday life 137
Outdoor adventures 193

Word cartoons 233
Index 237
Credits 248
Guide for grown-ups 252

GET TO KNOW YOUR VOCABULARY BOOK

WHAT'S ON THE PAGE?

Definition

Core word

sleep
close your eyes and rest
moonlit
night
expansive
window
occupied
bed
glorious
day
drawn
curtains
wake up
stop sleeping
functional
bedside
table

CAN YOU FIND BOGART?

Bogart the worm is often hiding inside this book. Can you find him?

WORD PAIRS

These are words that our data says commonly appear alongside each main word—and they make them even more epic!

WORD CARTOONS

We've turned some of our illustrations into mini cartoons! Turn to the back of the book to see what there is for you to watch.

adjust
p163
challenge
p200
design
p92
devour
p147
drowsy
p152
flush
p155
gargle
p51
gulp
p213
234

QR CODE

Simply scan the QR code with the camera on your smartphone or tablet. Some devices will require a QR scanner to do this. This can be downloaded for free from your app store of choice. If you have any trouble, you can find more detailed instructions at mrswordsmith.com.

WORDS FOR
EPIC ME

My Body

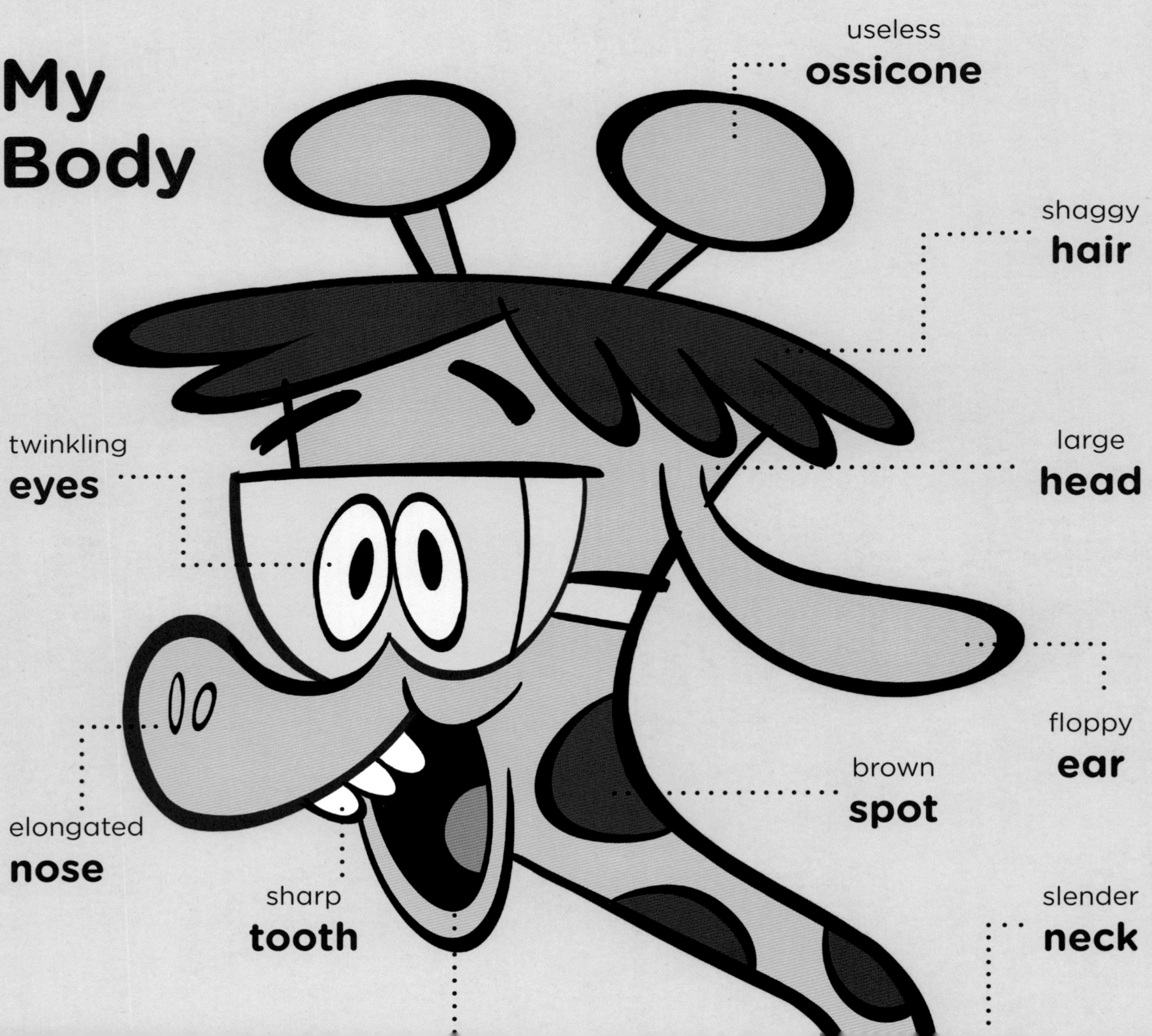
useless
ossicone
shaggy
hair
twinkling
eyes
large
head
floppy
ear
brown
spot
elongated
nose
sharp
tooth
slender
neck

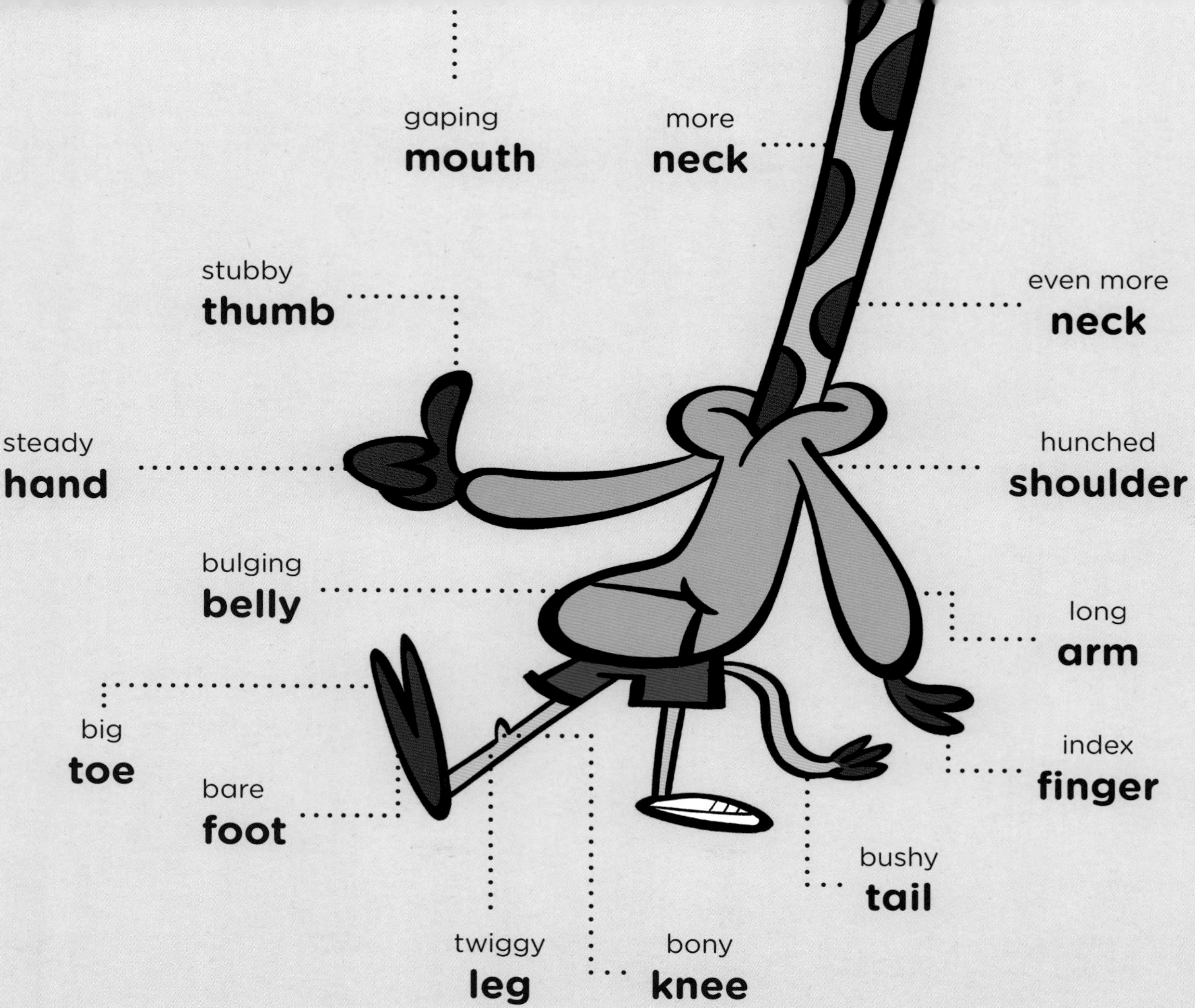
gaping mouth
more neck
stubby thumb
even more neck
steady hand
hunched shoulder
bulging belly
long arm
big toe
index finger
bare foot
bushy tail
twiggy leg
bony knee

ALL YOU NEED IS...

love

deep caring
and affection

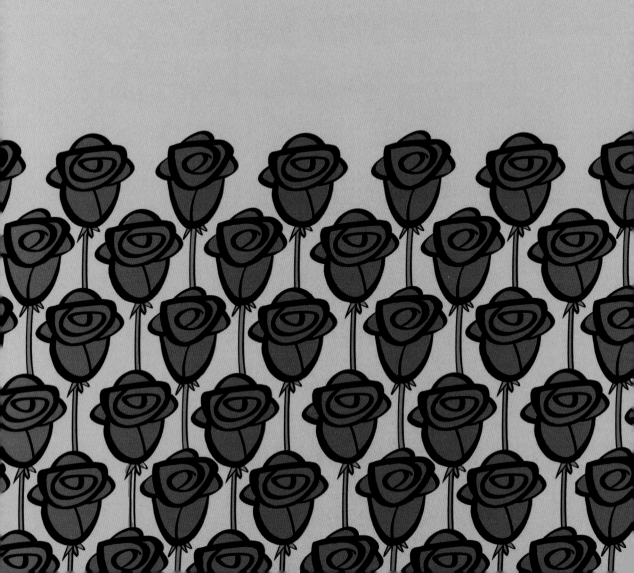

unique

the only one of its kind

nonconformist

someone who doesn't do things like everyone else

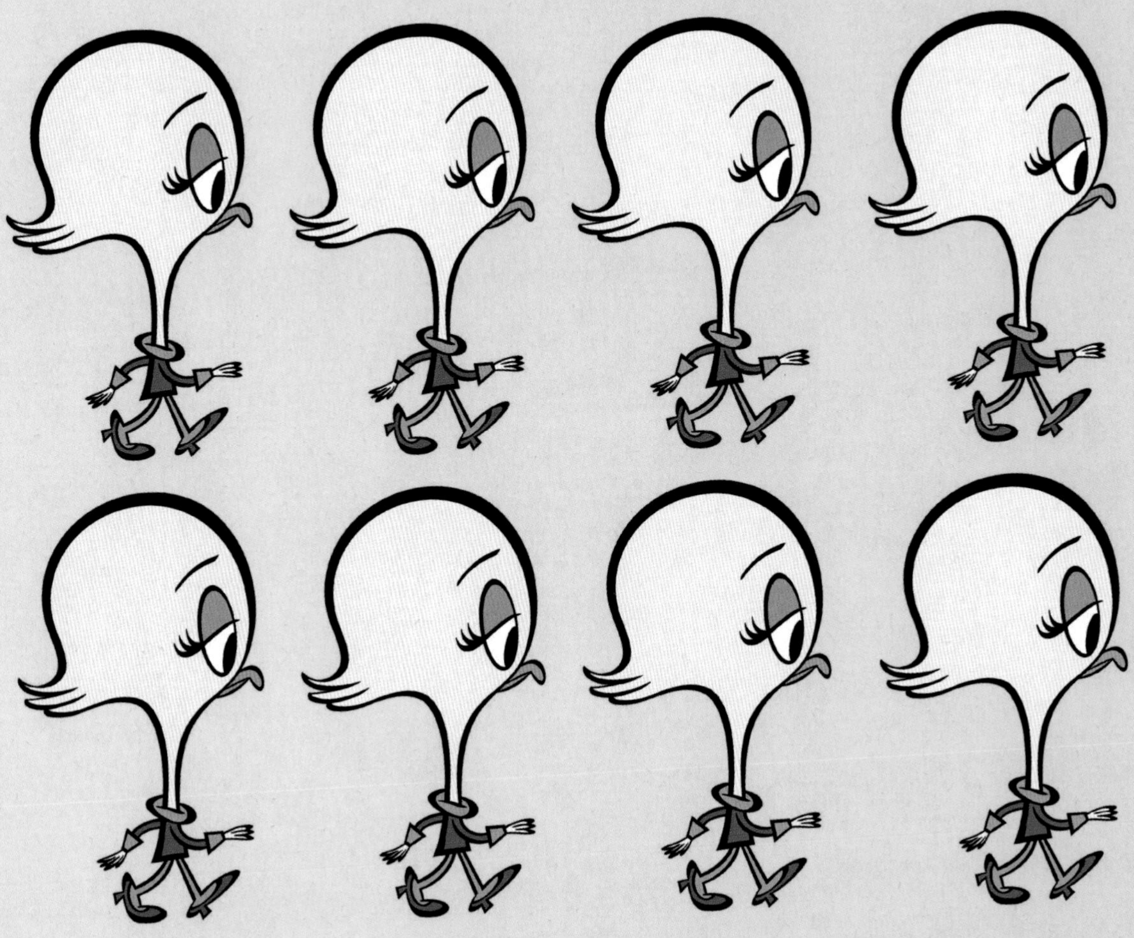

friends

people who get along well
and love each other

friendship
bracelets

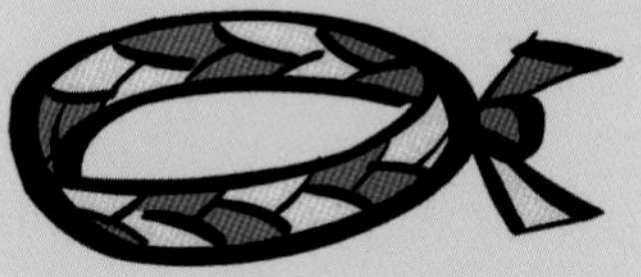

adventurous
friend

true
friend

best
friends

old
friend

family
friend

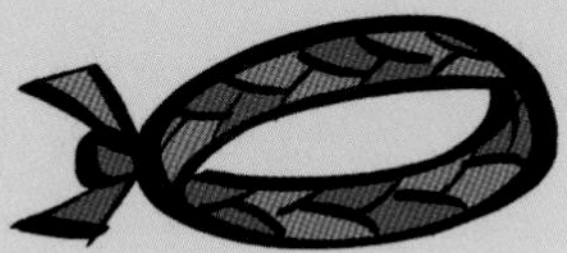

new
friend

respect

treat others with appreciation and behave politely

polite

behaving in a respectful way

sob

cry noisily with loud gasps

LET IT
ALL OUT

cry

get teary because you are so emotional

wail

cry out with a long, high noise

blubber

cry uncontrollably and loudly

I'M
HERE
FOR YOU

comfort

soothe someone and
make them feel better

sympathetic

understanding how somebody feels and comforting them

pity

a feeling of sadness
for someone else

relate

understand someone because of something in common

mischievous

naughty and playful

ONE HAND IN
THE COOKIE JAR

blame

say that something
is someone's fault

ZZZ

forgive

stop feeling angry
with someone

playful
laughing
happy
cheerful
goofy

glum
confused
upset
angry
sad

include

let everyone join in

exclude

leave someone out

BEARNICE VS. THE TICKLE TWINS

laughing

howling

hysterical

unable to control yourself

NOT IN THE MOOD

frown

look sad with your
eyebrows pushed down

pout

stick your lips out
in a moody way

scowl

frown in an angry
or bad-tempered way

sulk

be quiet and grumpy

HAPPY
BIRTHDAY

enormous
present

bashful

shy and nervous
around others

rotating
disco ball
flickering
candles
lucky
birthday boy
birthday
cake

lucky
birthday girl

squeal
make a long,
high-pitched noise

festive
flags
dangling
piñata

try

make an effort
to do something

WORDS FOR
TIME

BRUSH YOUR TEETH FO
2 MINUTES

30 seconds
60 seconds
90 seconds
cutting-edge
hoverboard

gargle

make a funny noise as you wash your mouth and throat

minty
toothpaste

2 minutes

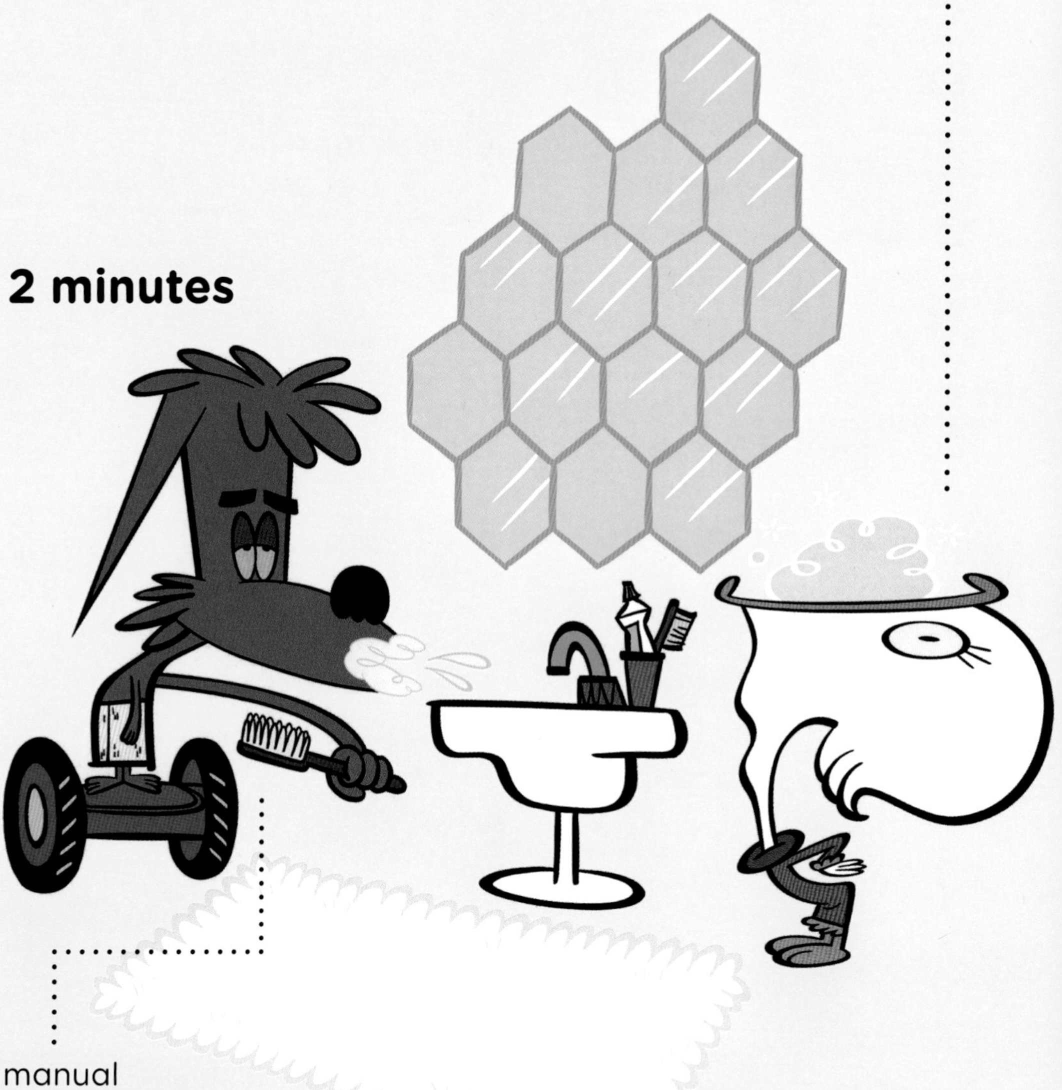

manual
toothbrush

DAYS OF THE WEEK

bone
Monday

chickenless bone bucket
Thursday

basic bone broth
Friday

bone burger

Tuesday

bones on toast

Wednesday

bone cone

Saturday

supersize bone

Sunday

Months of the Year

January

February

March

July

August

September

One year. No washing. No haircuts. Go!

April

May

June

October

November

December

A Worm for All Seasons

spring
summer

winter
fall

The Chinese Zodiac

rat

1

ox

tiger

horse

goat

monkey

I was born in the Year of the…

rabbit

dragon

snake

rooster

dog

pig

WORDS FOR
NUMBERS, SHAPES, AND SIZES

COUNTING
IN FIVES

impressive

really good or awesome

five doughnuts

ten doughnuts

fifteen doughnuts

twenty doughnuts

regret

feel bad and wish
you hadn't done something

...twenty-five doughnuts

DONUTS

COUNTING IN 10s

ten

twenty

thirty

forty

fifty

sixty

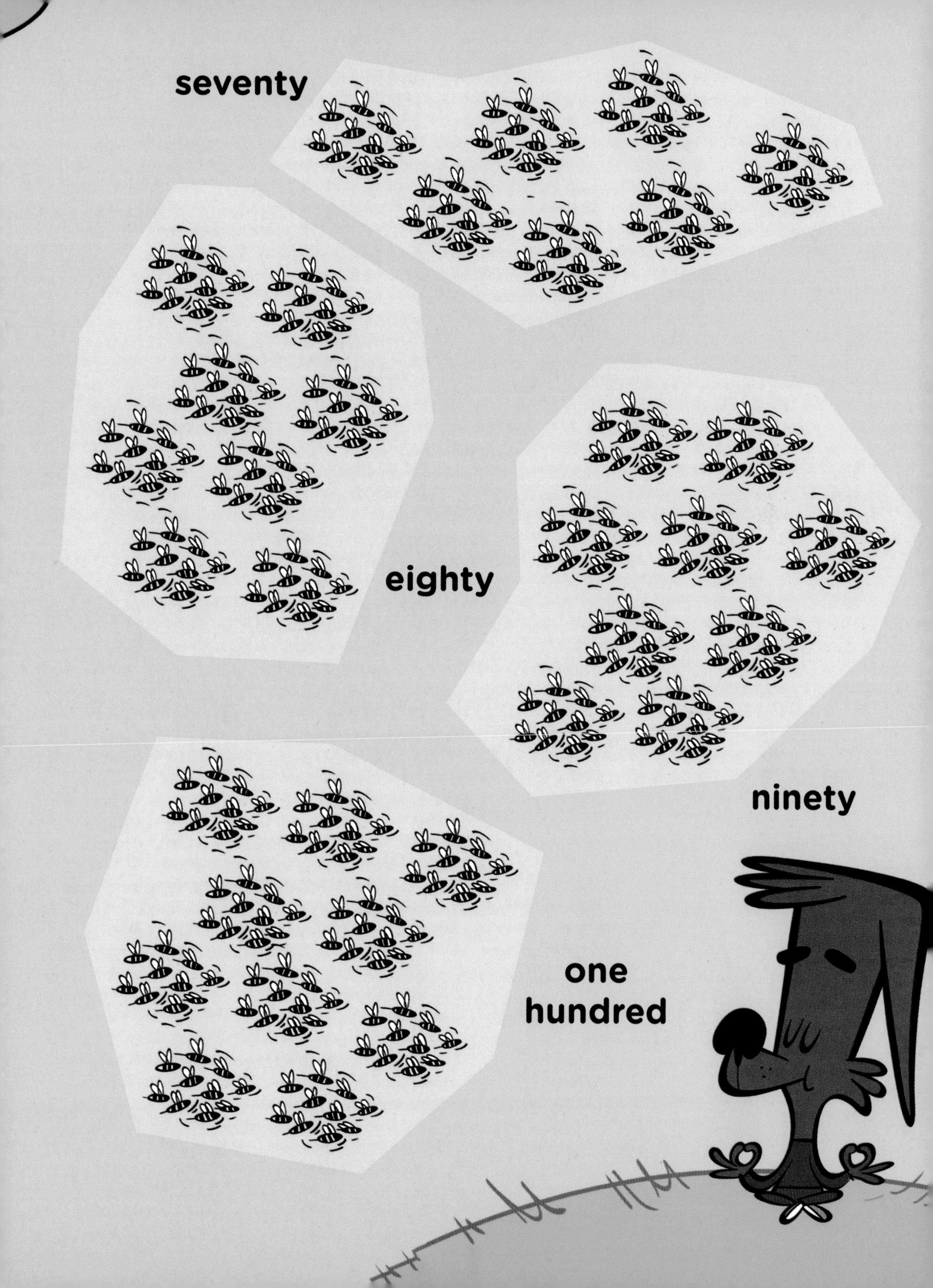
seventy
eighty
ninety
one hundred

SHAPES

square circle triangle

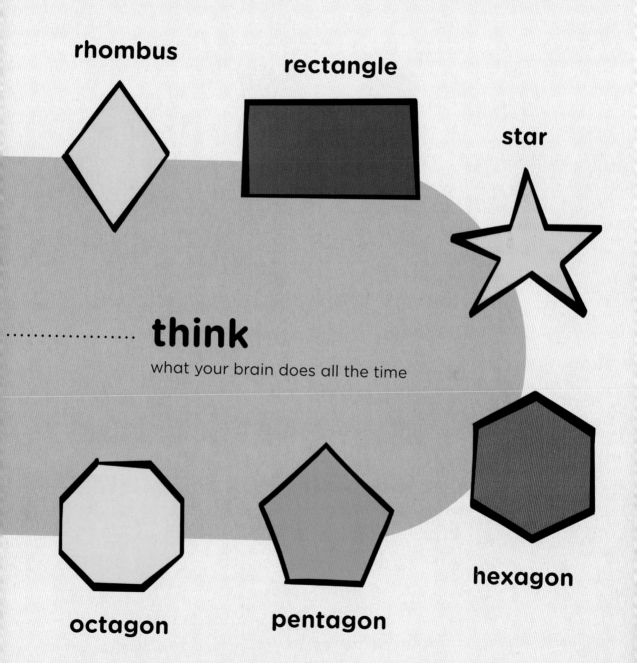

rhombus

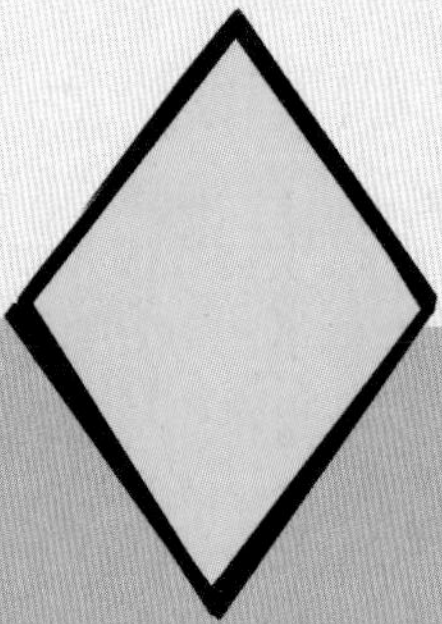

rectangle

star

think

what your brain does all the time

hexagon

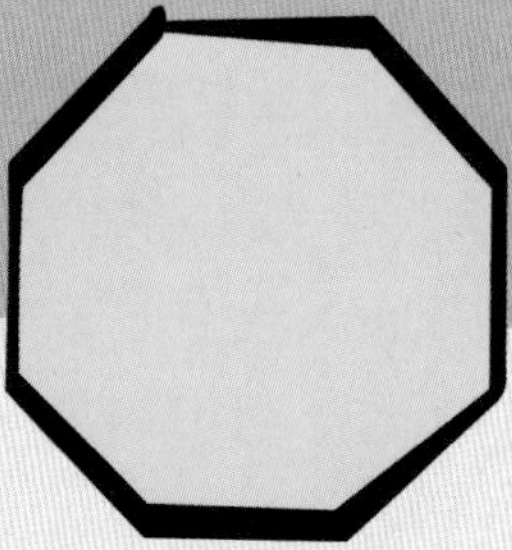

octagon

pentagon

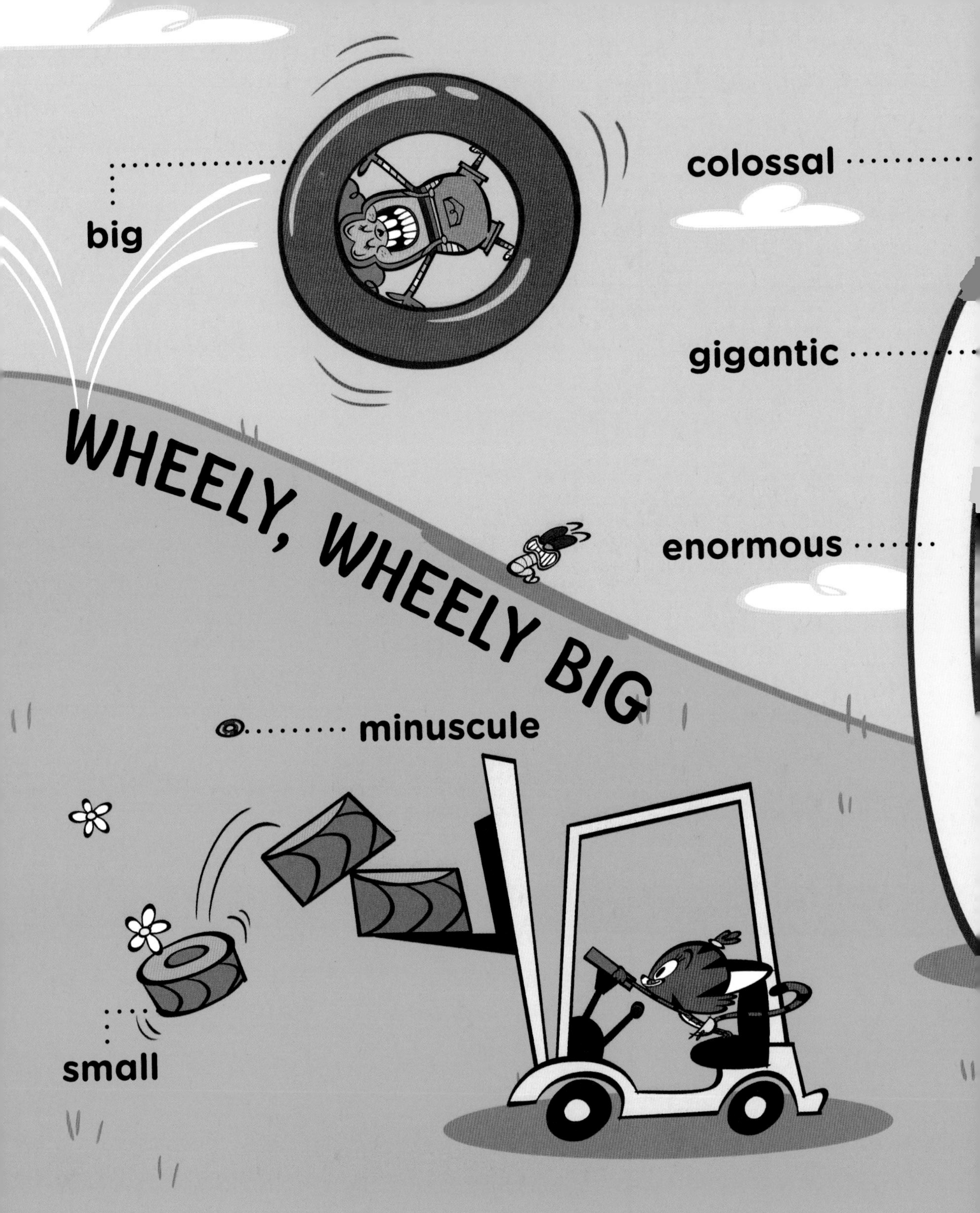
WHEELY, WHEELY BIG
big
colossal
gigantic
enormous
minuscule
small

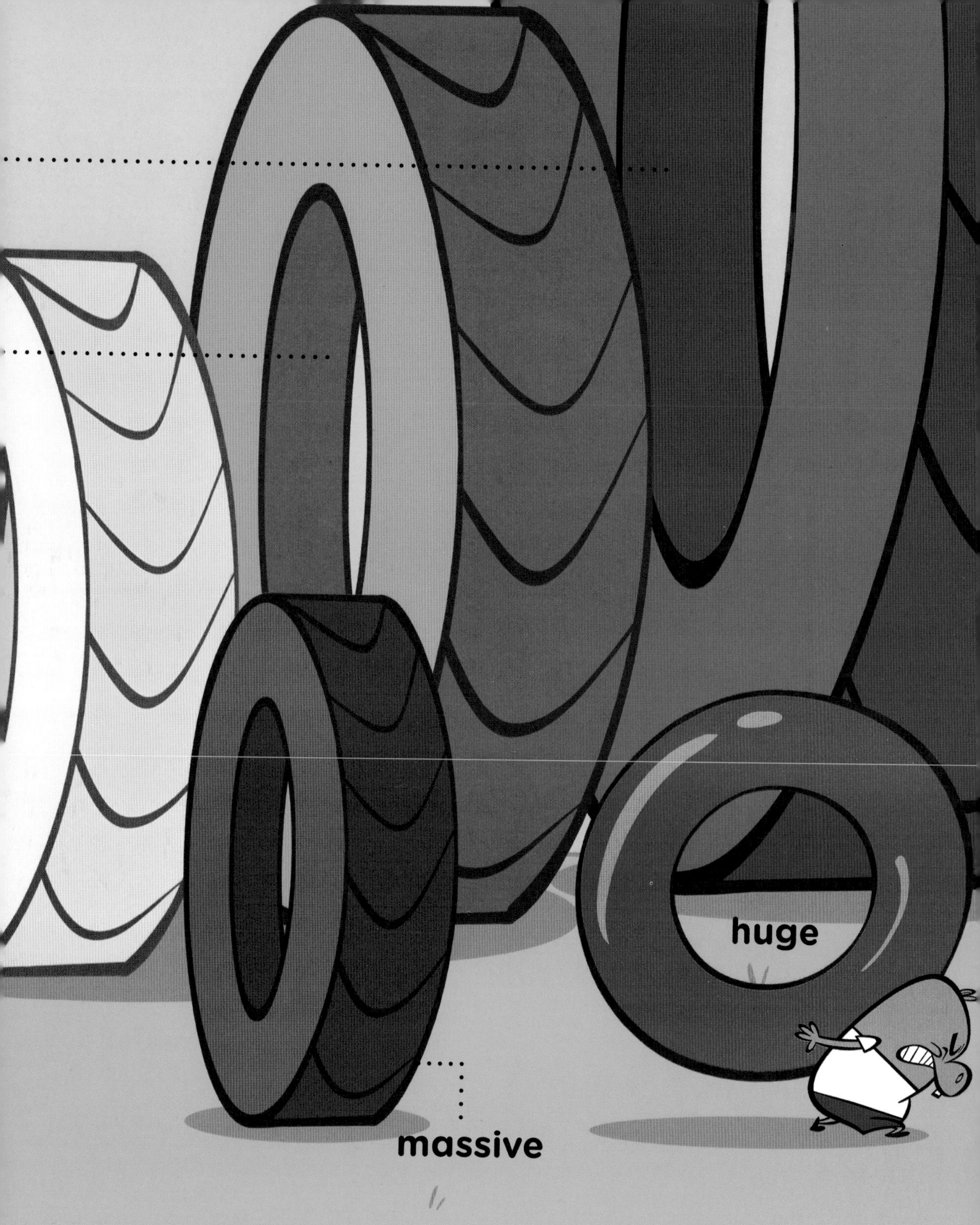
huge
massive

Don't look down

soaring

high

vertigo

the dizzy feeling of losing balance when you look down from high up

towering

lofty

share

have or do something
with other people

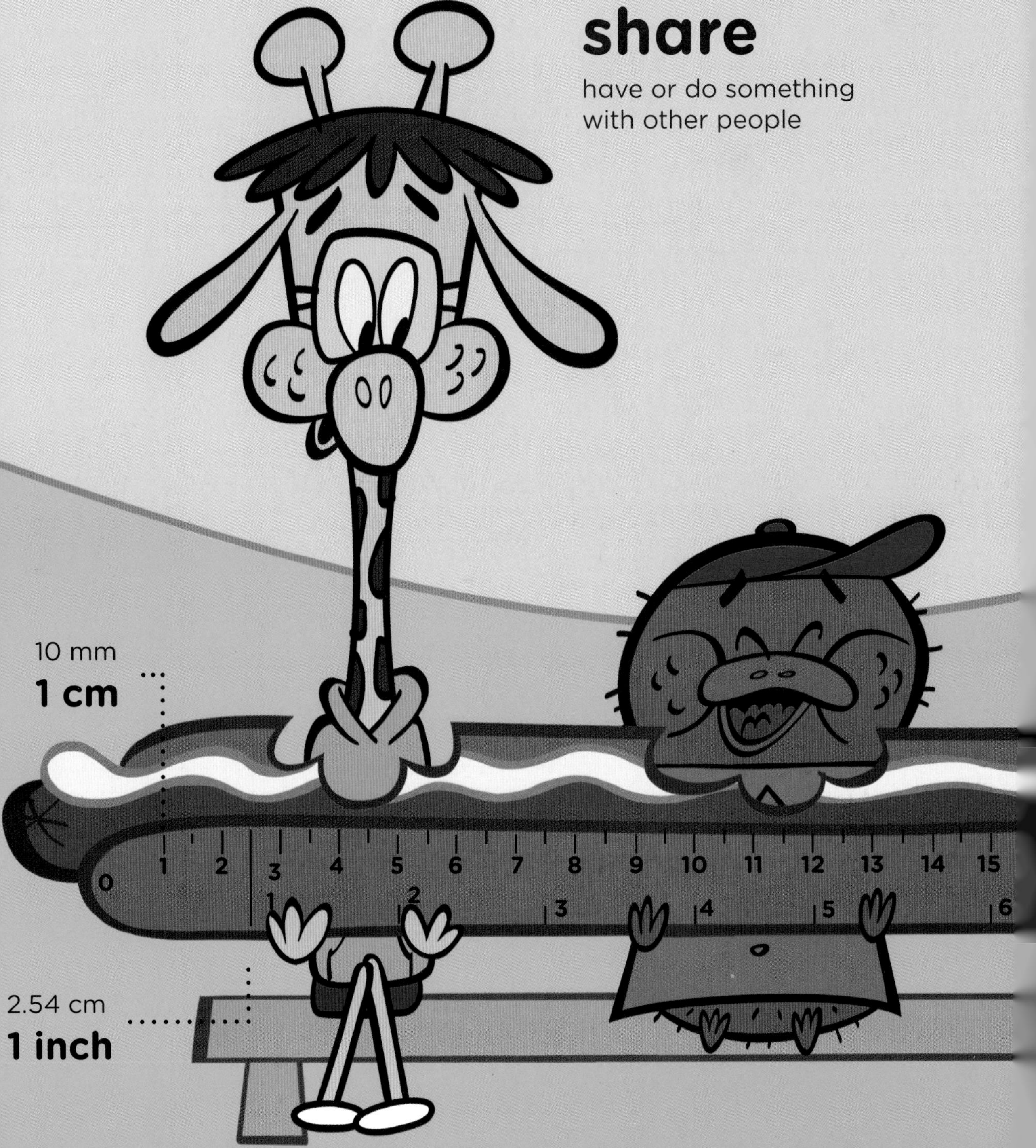

10 mm
1 cm
2.54 cm
1 inch

Footlong Hot Dog

17 18 19 20 21 22 23 24 25 26 27 28 29 30
7 8 9 10 11 12

30.48 cm
12 inches
1 foot

WORDS FOR

WHERE AND HOW

on

in

beneath

behind

in front of

next to

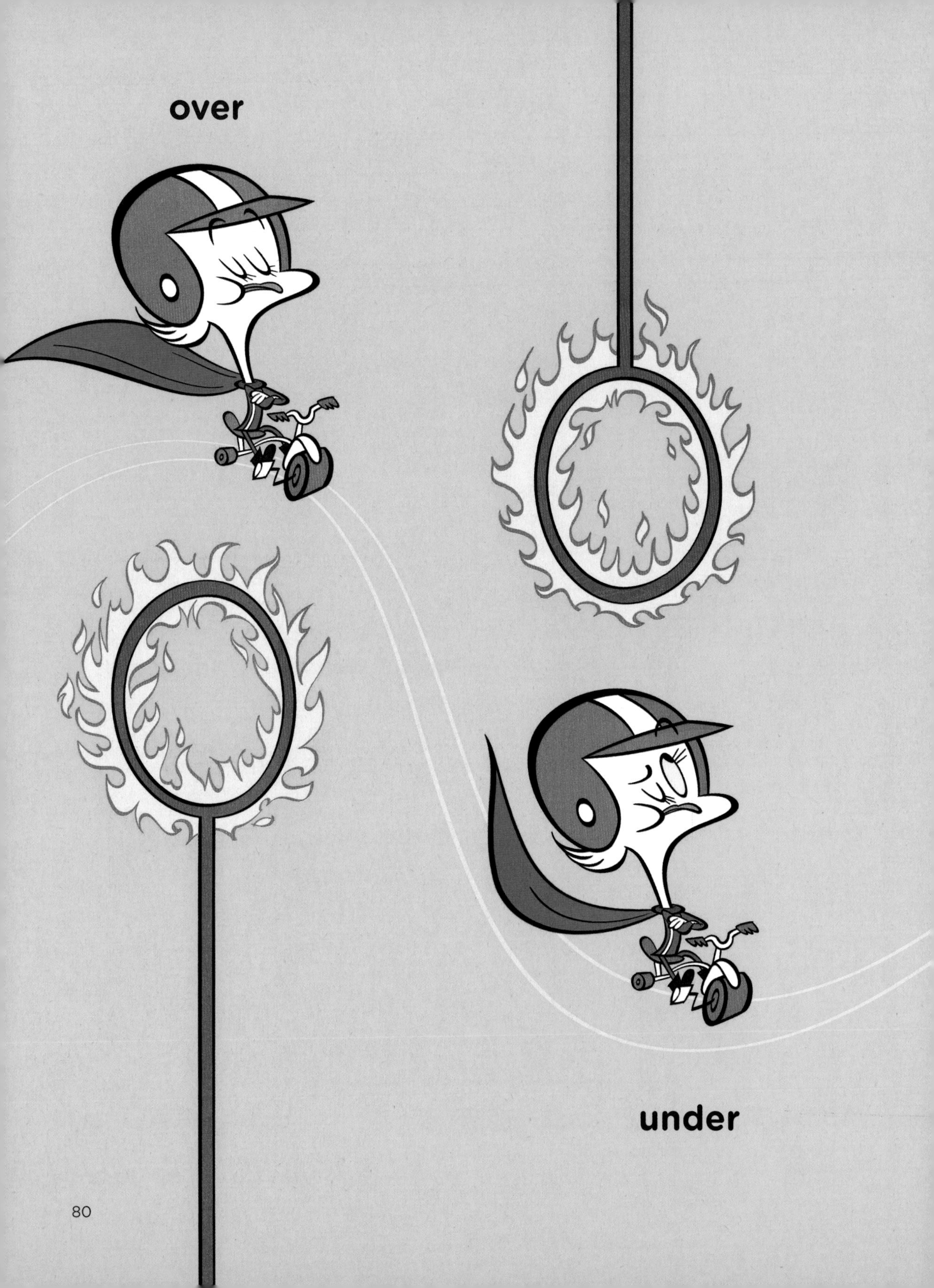
over
under

around

toasted

marshmallow

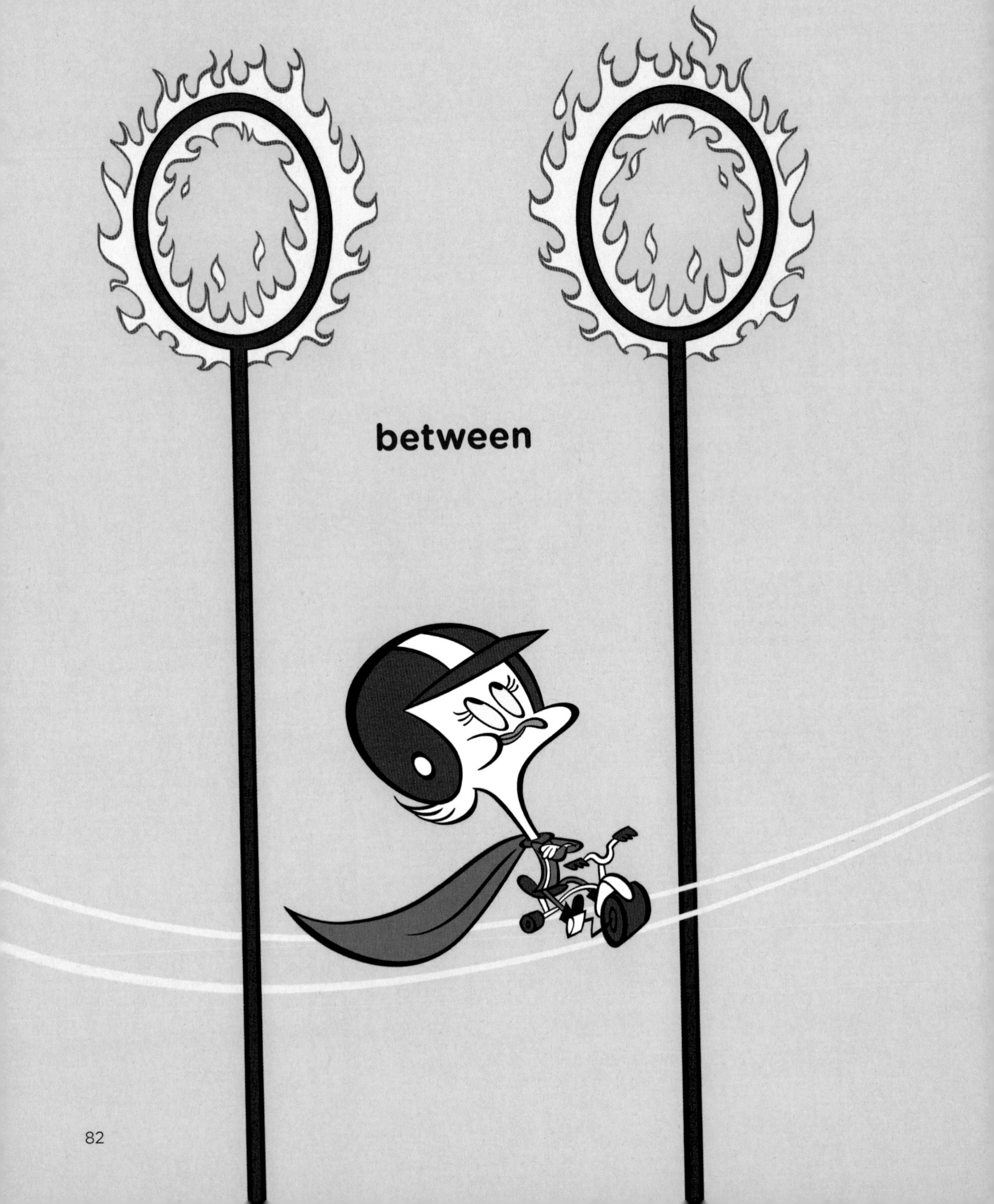

between

through

amazing

incredible or surprising

upside down

right side up

muddled

mixed up and the wrong way around

opposite

completely different in every way

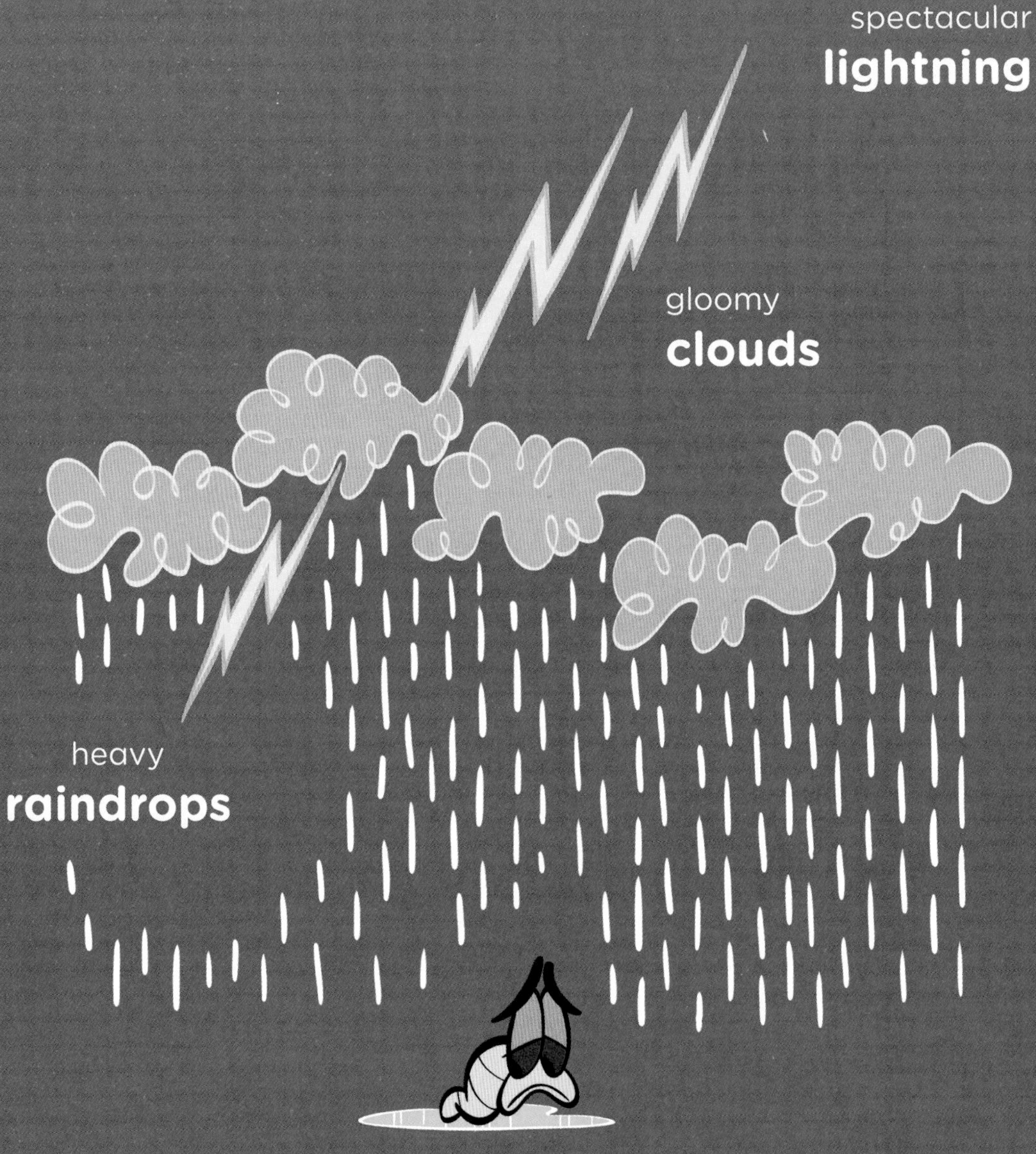
spectacular
lightning
gloomy
clouds
heavy
raindrops

opposite

completely different in every way

scorching

sun

wispy

clouds

golden

sunshine

WORDS FOR
TECHNOLOGY

DARE TO BE DIFFERENT

YOU WERE BORN TO MAKE A DIFFERENCE

BUILD
YOUR OWN
BEAR

need

want something that
is important to you

design

plan to make something

rough
sketch

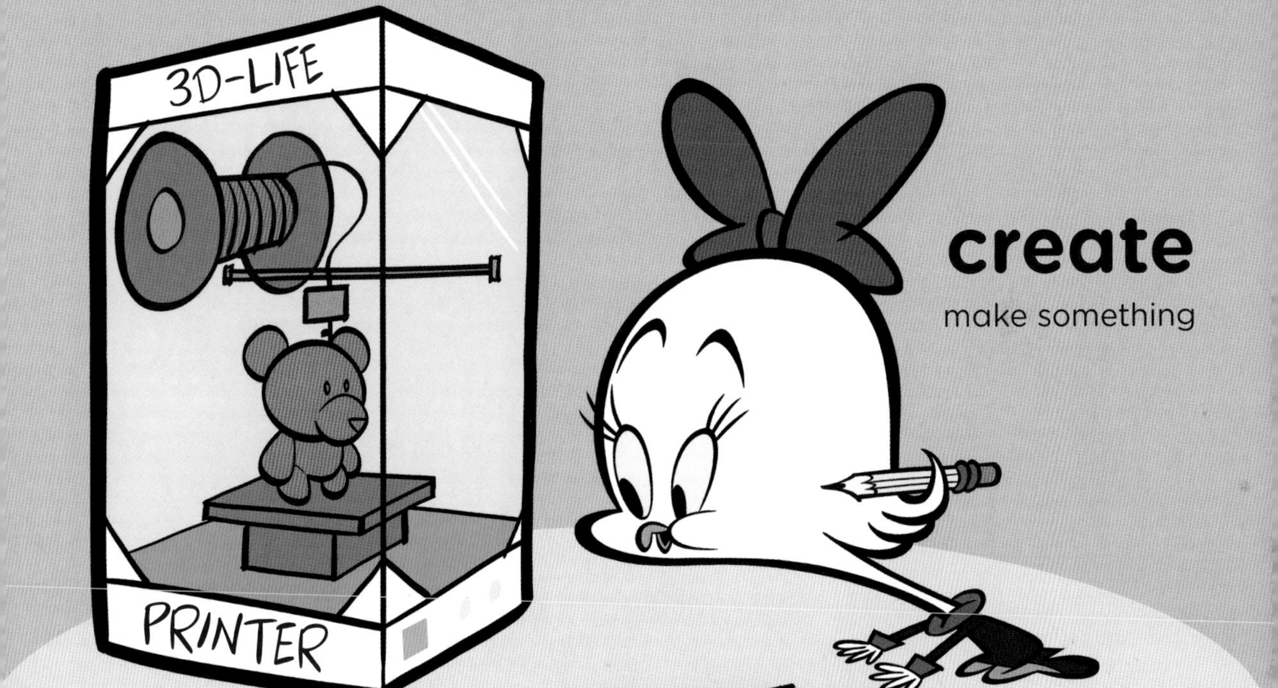
3D-LIFE
PRINTER

create

make something

incredible
3D printer

ambitious
blueprint

OZ'S PUPPY FASHION
beautiful
crystal
light-speed
space racer
glazed
doughnut
extravagant
lobster
gourmet
burger

wear

have clothes on your body

swaggering
cowboy
complex
circuit board
fierce
tiger
steamed
bun
fried
egg

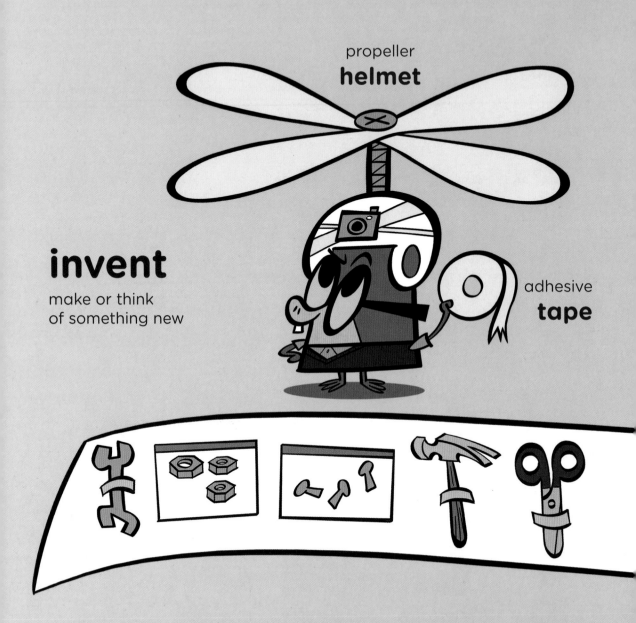

propeller
helmet

invent

make or think
of something new

adhesive
tape

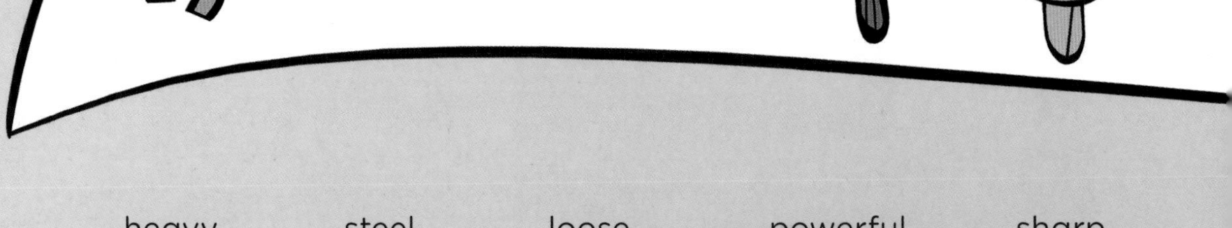

heavy
wrench

steel
nuts

loose
bolts

powerful
hammer

sharp
scissors

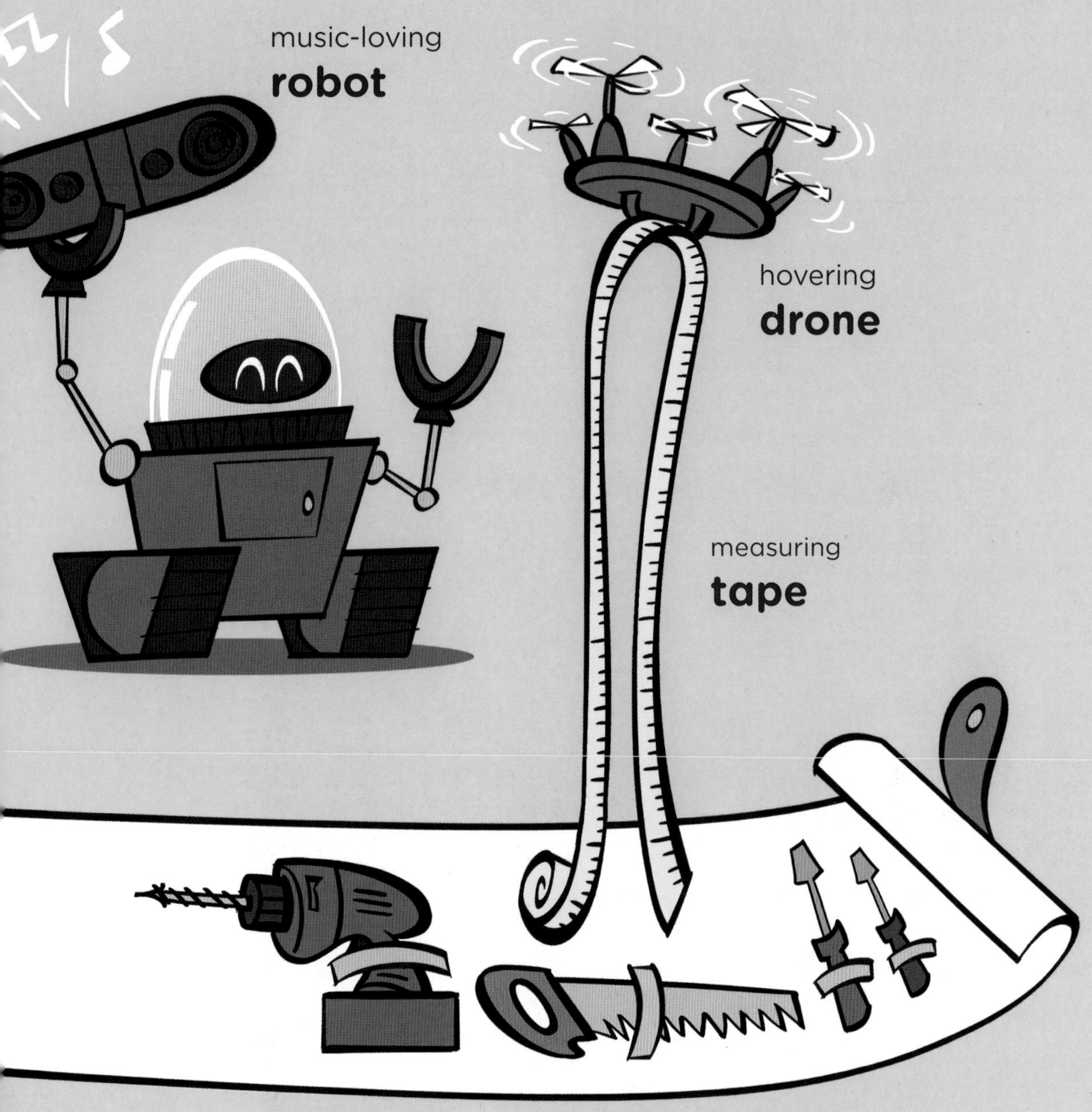
music-loving
robot
hovering
drone
measuring
tape
electric
drill
jagged
saw
simple
screwdrivers

Scooter Workshop

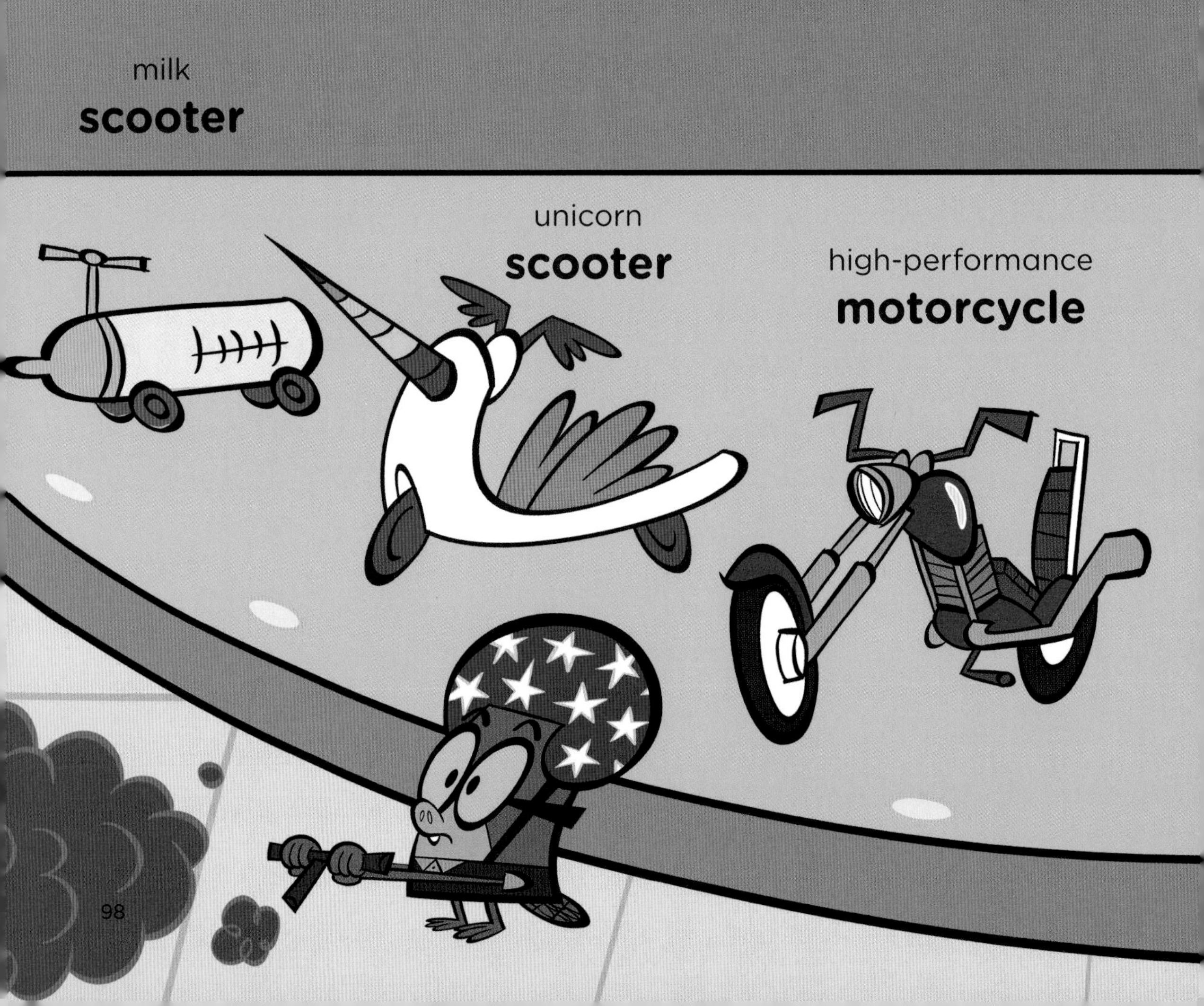

milk
scooter
unicorn
scooter
high-performance
motorcycle

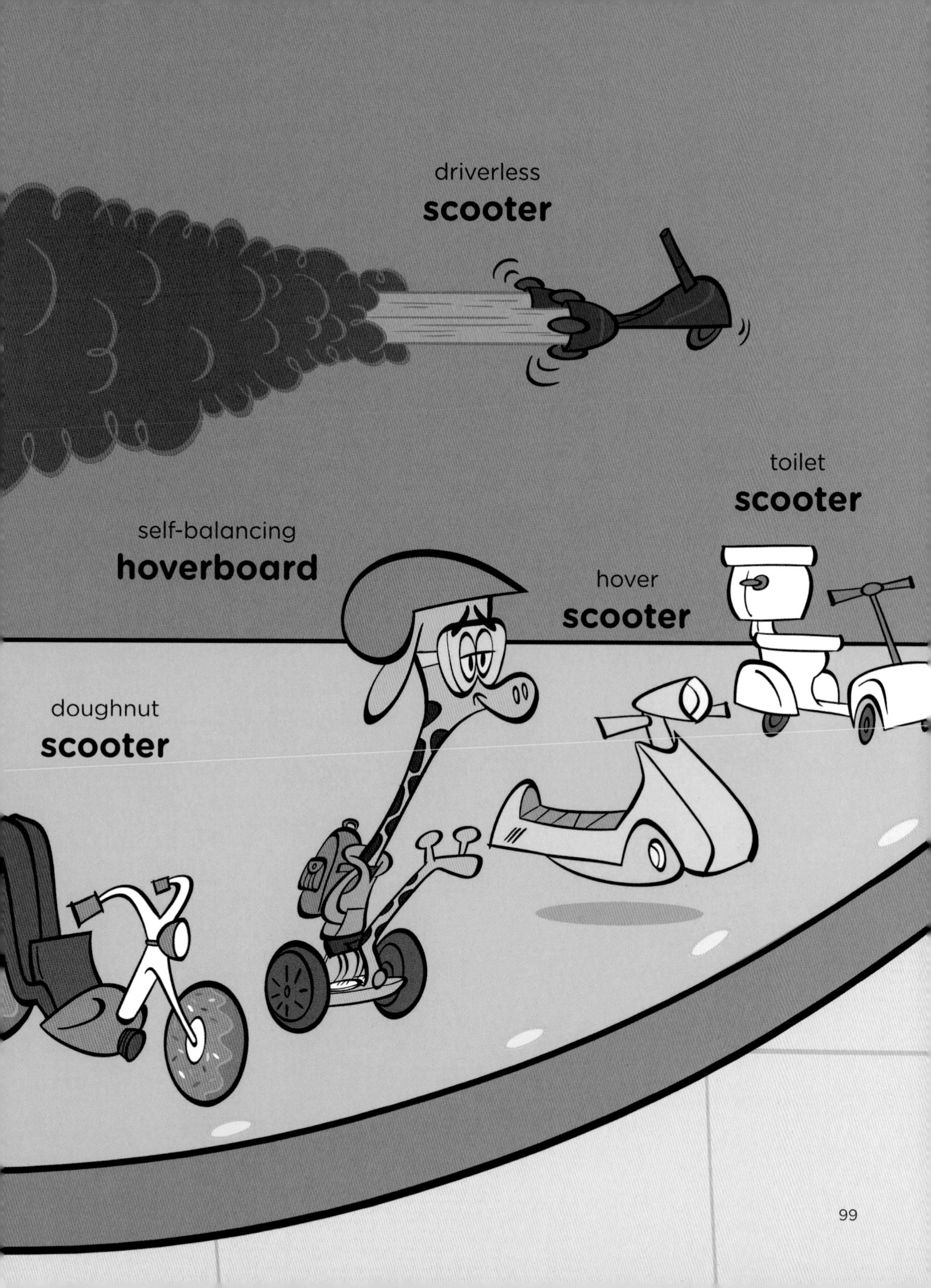
driverless
scooter
toilet
scooter
self-balancing
hoverboard
hover
scooter
doughnut
scooter

enthusiastic

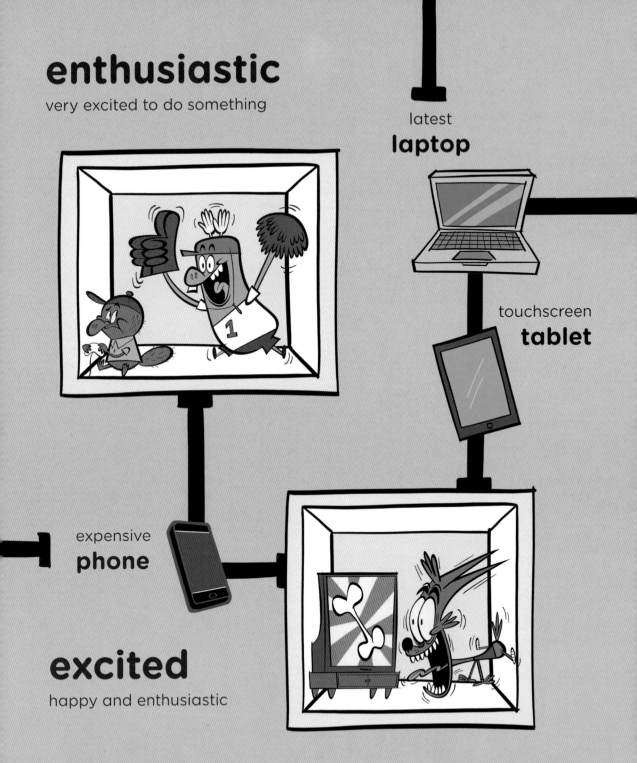

very excited to do something

latest **laptop**

touchscreen **tablet**

expensive **phone**

excited

happy and enthusiastic

obsessed

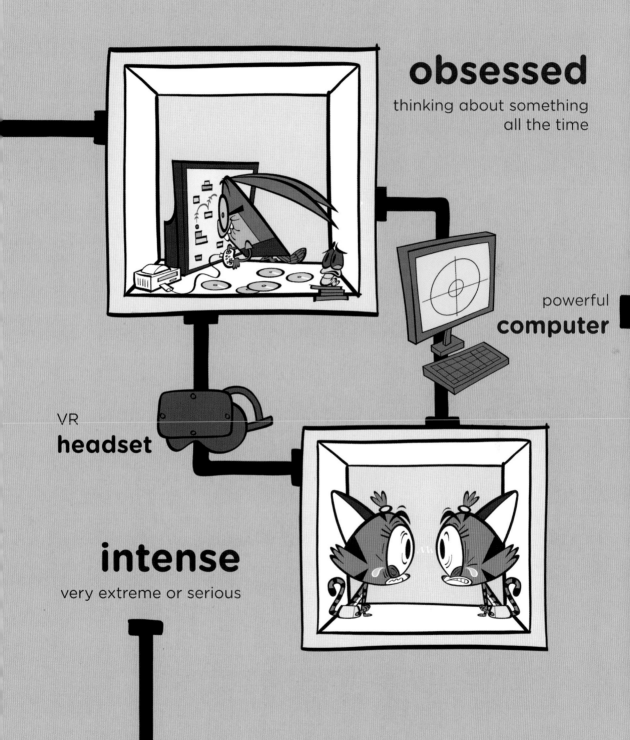

thinking about something all the time

powerful **computer**

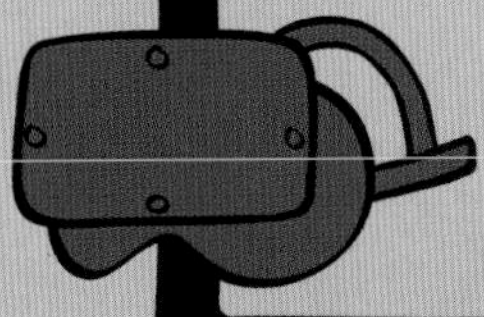

VR **headset**

intense

very extreme or serious

HOW TO MAKE A VIDEO GAME

1UP

game designer

dreams up the video game

producer

makes sure everything is going to plan

user interface designer

plans how the game will look

researcher

finds information to make the game better

y

writer

creates the story and world of the game

DICTIONARY

concept artist

draws the world, characters, and objects in the game

game tester

plays the game to make sure it works

programmer

writes the code to make the game work

animator

makes the game move like a cartoon

WORDS FOR
LEARNING AND CREATING

DO YOU READ ME?
read a novel
read
look at and understand
read a book

read a
newspaper
The Word
PEACE ACHIEVE
read a
map
read
minds
WORD-O's
read a
cereal box
read an
email
read
body
language

inspire

make someone excited to do something

difficult

not easy

dinosaur
puzzle

furious

very angry or raging

tricky

needing lots of skill or practice

airborne
juggling clubs

scattered
playing cards

THAT'S CHEATING, BRICK!

problem

something that you need to fix or solve

shortcut

a quicker or easier way of doing something

solution

a way to fix or solve a problem

ARTY PARTY

paint

make a picture with paint

spotless

apron

insulted

how you feel when someone does something you find rude

wooden
easel
taut
canvas

sculpt

make shapes out
of something like
stone or clay

masterpiece

an amazing work of art

passion

a very powerful feeling

scribbled
picture
white
chalk
thick
paintbrush
waterproof
glue
moist
clay

hand-painted
mural
waxy
crayons
metallic
spray paint
spilled
glitter

electric
purple
candy apple
red
lemon
yellow
emerald
green
millennial
pink
sky
blue
eggshell
white

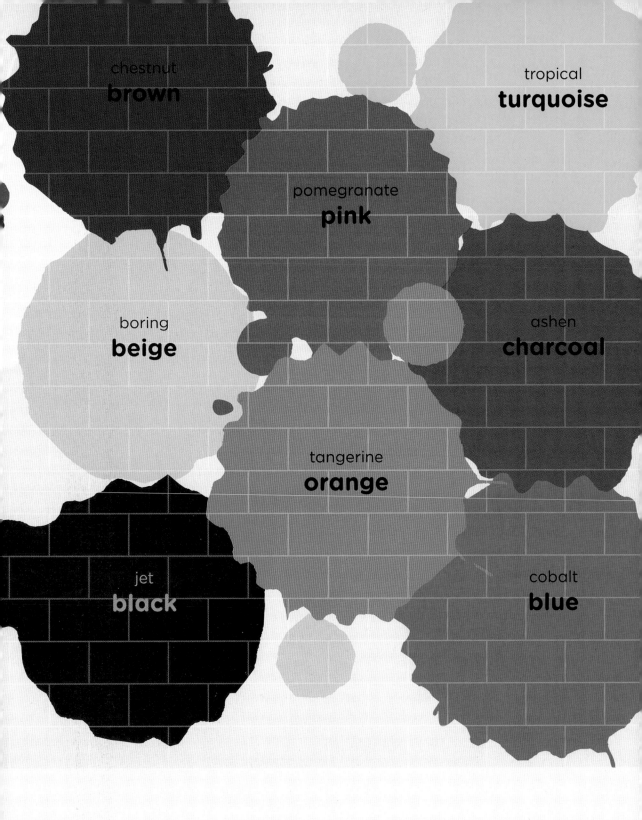

chestnut
brown

tropical
turquoise

pomegranate
pink

boring
beige

ashen
charcoal

tangerine
orange

jet
black

cobalt
blue

good
better

practice

doing something again and
again to get better at it

best

skip

move lightly on foot
with a hop and a jump

crawl

move on your
hands and knees

walk

move on foot at a normal speed

LOOK BOTH WAYS
STOP

run

move quickly on foot

tangled
earphones
bulky
pencil
case

spiky
compass

handy
calculator

reusable
water bottle

Rule the School

influence

change the way other people act

Good
Dog

write

make words or letters

focus

think about something
without getting distracted

empower

give someone the ability
to do something

WORDS FOR

EVERYDAY LIFE

neat

arranged in a tidy and ordered way

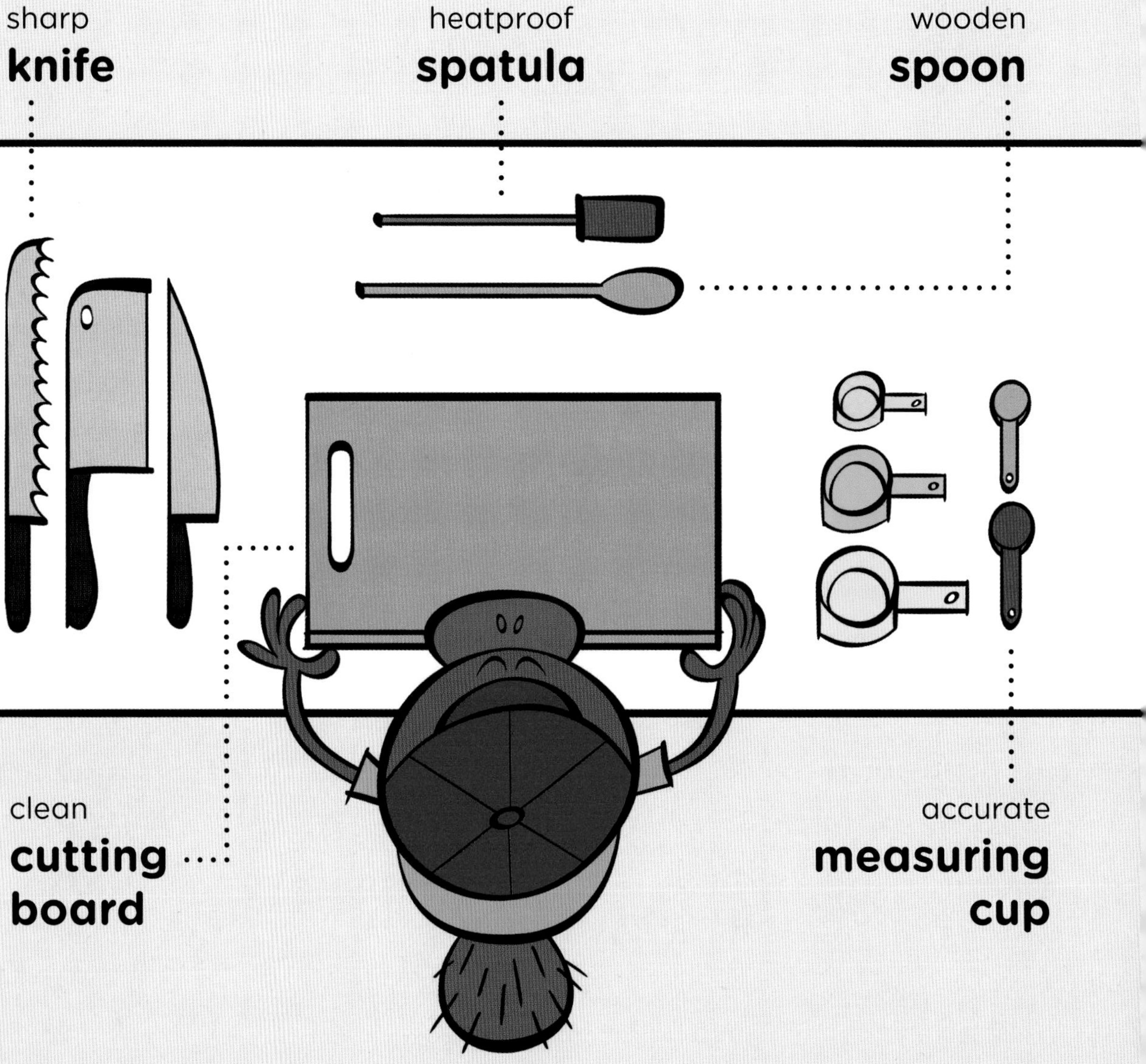
sharp
knife
heatproof
spatula
wooden
spoon
clean
cutting board
accurate
measuring cup

serving
spoon

metal
spatula

handheld
whisk

folded
napkin

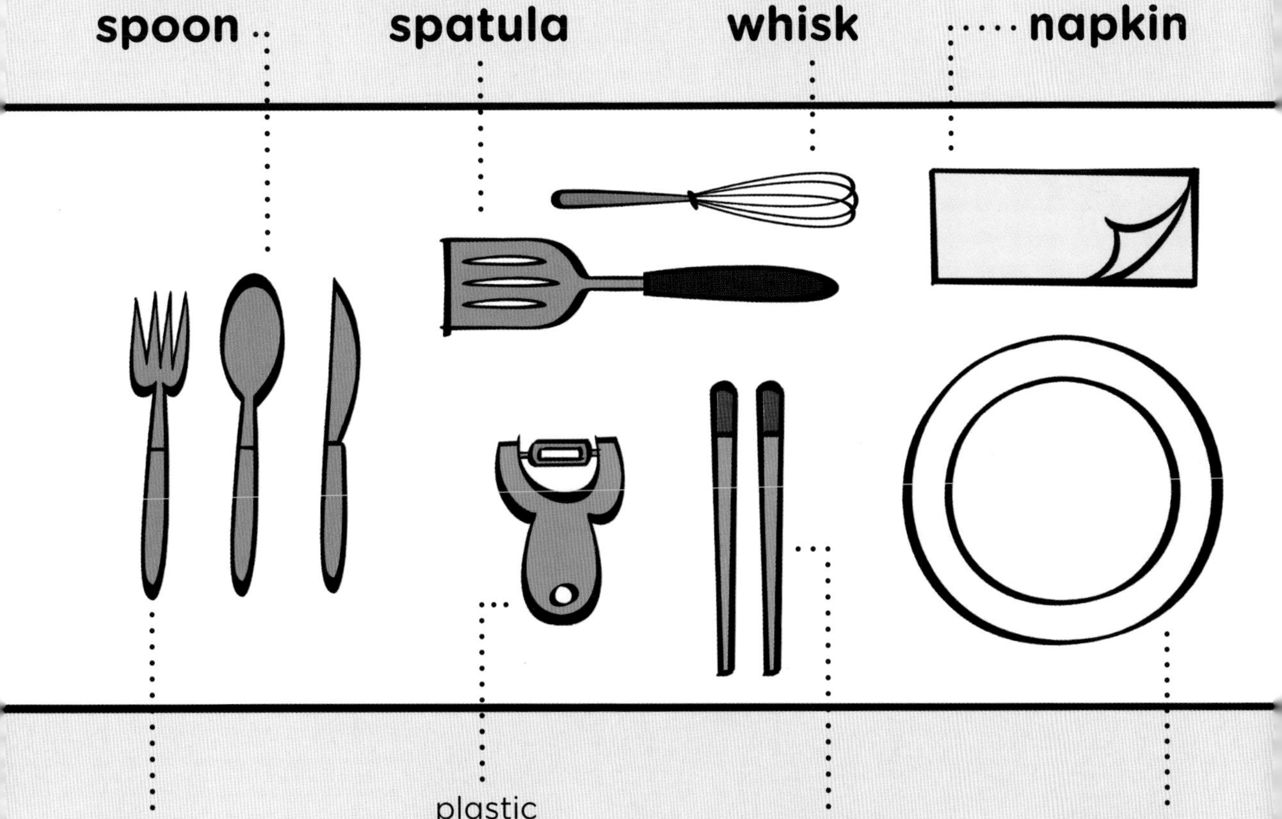

silver
fork

plastic
potato peeler

elegant
chopsticks

ceramic
plate

1
large
onion

2
raw
ginger

3
leftover
ham

4
free-range
chicken

13
aromatic
herbs

5
juicy
shrimp

6
organic
beef

7
creamy
butter

8
silken
tofu

9
crunchy
celery

10
peppery
radish

1
2
3
4
5
6
7
8
9
10
11
12

11
organic
carrot

12
fresh
cabbage

22
healthy
sweet potato

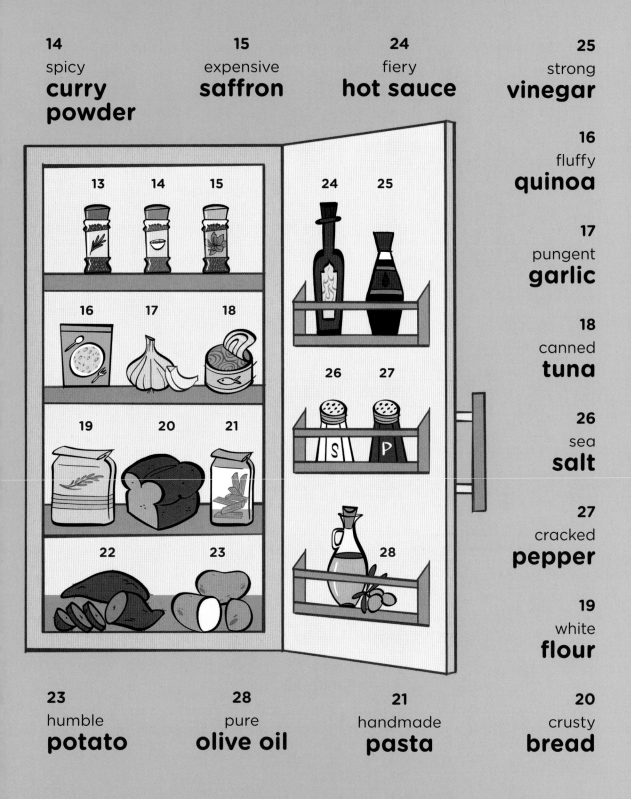

14
spicy
curry powder

15
expensive
saffron

24
fiery
hot sauce

25
strong
vinegar

16
fluffy
quinoa

17
pungent
garlic

18
canned
tuna

26
sea
salt

27
cracked
pepper

19
white
flour

13
14
15
24
25
16
17
18
26
27
S
P
19
20
21
28
22
23

23
humble
potato

28
pure
olive oil

21
handmade
pasta

20
crusty
bread

In the mood for food?

hungry

wanting or needing food

empty
bowl

starving

very, very hungry

sesame seed
bun

steamed
broccoli

reject

strongly say no
to something

What's Cooking?

soaring
pancake

eager
really wanting to do something

cast-iron
griddle

robotic
chef
nonstick
skillet
sizzling
frying pan
heavy
lid
red-hot
stove
stainless-steel
saucepan

Come 'n' get it!
nibble
take tiny bites of something
tasty
bones
ceramic
mug
unwanted
leftovers
hemp
bib

eat

put something in your mouth and swallow it

stylish
dining table

scrumptious
pies
sturdy
chair

devour

eat quickly and greedily

succulent
kebab

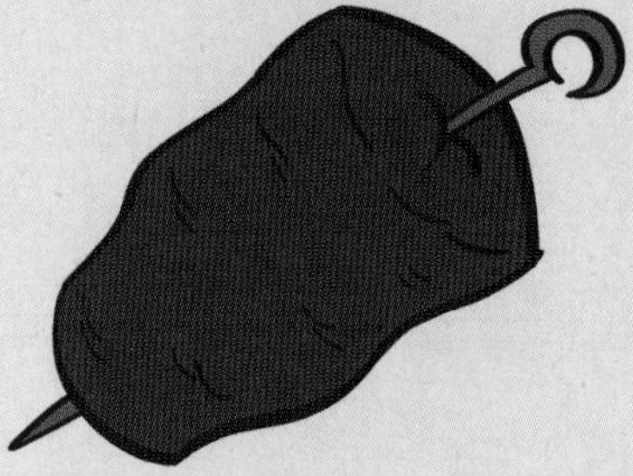

steamed
dumplings

footlong
hot dog

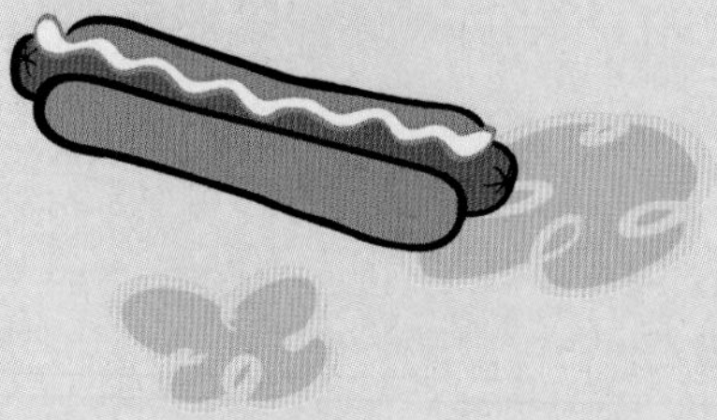

PLATO'S
TACOS
PT
PT
TAC01

authentic
taco

wood-fired
pizza

sticky
noodles

LUNCH RUSH

healthy
salad

hand-rolled
sushi

classic
burger

shriek
make a short, loud cry

MILK BAR

plump
blueberry

fuzzy
kiwi

luscious
strawberry

rosy
apple

hand-picked
grape

overripe
banana

tropical
coconut

organic
pear

refreshing
watermelon

sour
lemon

tangy
orange

that's not a
banana

MILK

awake

not sleeping

yawning

taking a big, tired breath

drowsy

tired and about
to fall asleep

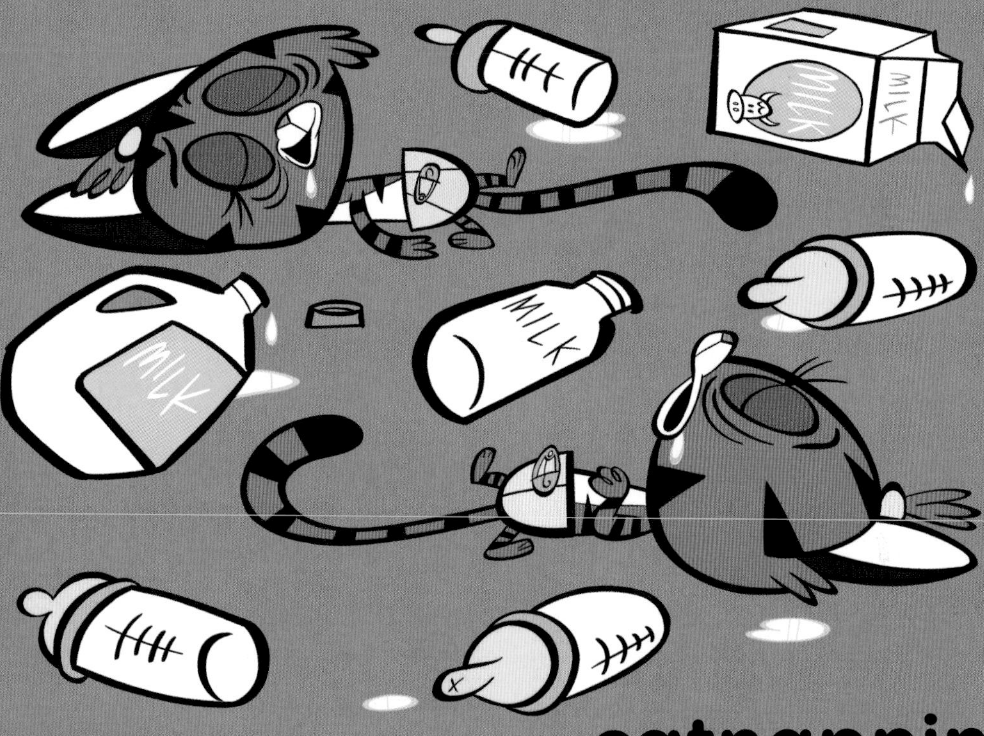
MILK
MILK
MILK
MILK

catnapping

sleeping during the day

Take the Plunge!

unroll

unwind or unwrap

quilted

toilet paper

flush

empty the toilet
with water

overflowing
toilet

plastic
pipes

Wee-Wee-Woes

desperate

needing something very badly

secure
lock

flustered

confused and panicking

empty
roll

relief

the nice feeling when something unpleasant stops

portable
potty

Bath Time!

bubble
bath

ecstatic

full of joy or happiness

power
shower
free-standing
bathtub

miserable

unhappy or uncomfortable

CAT WASH!

wash

clean something with water

rainfall

shower head

lather

rinse

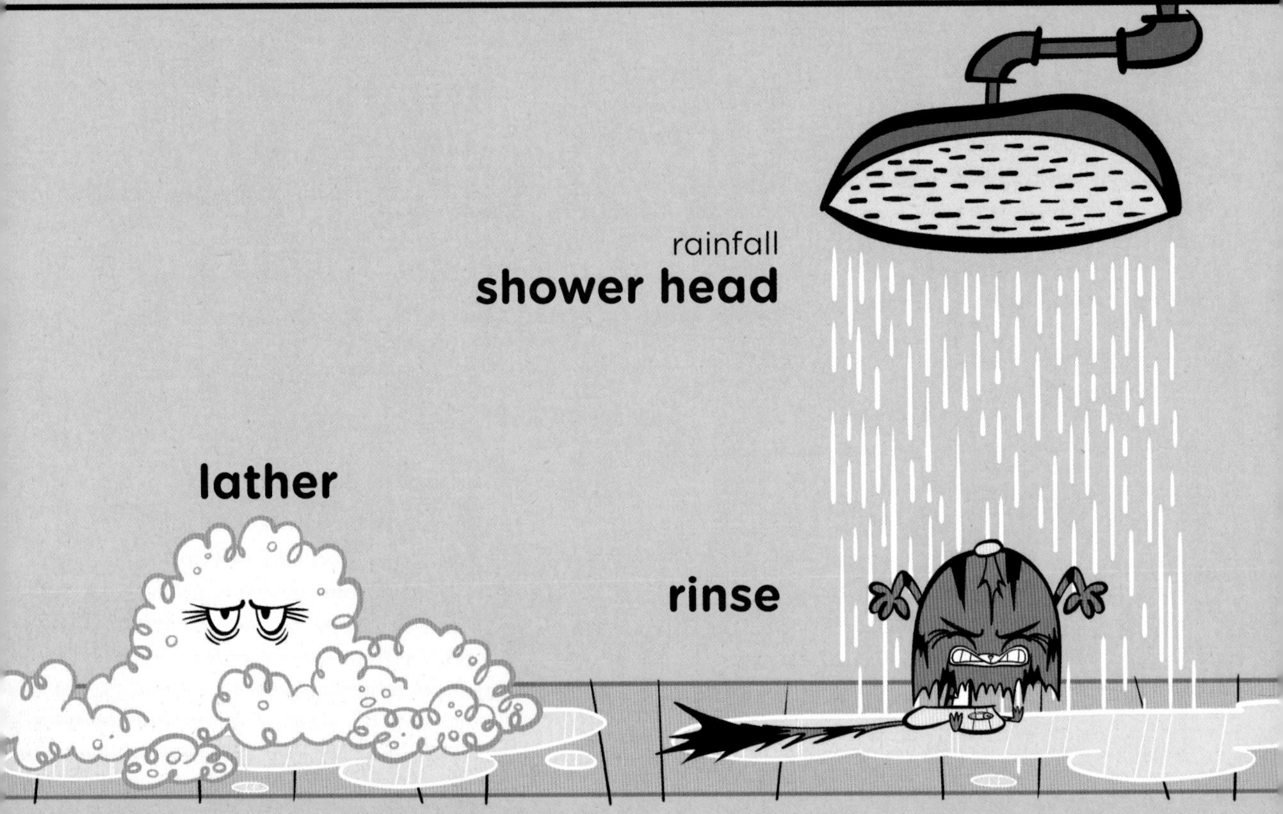

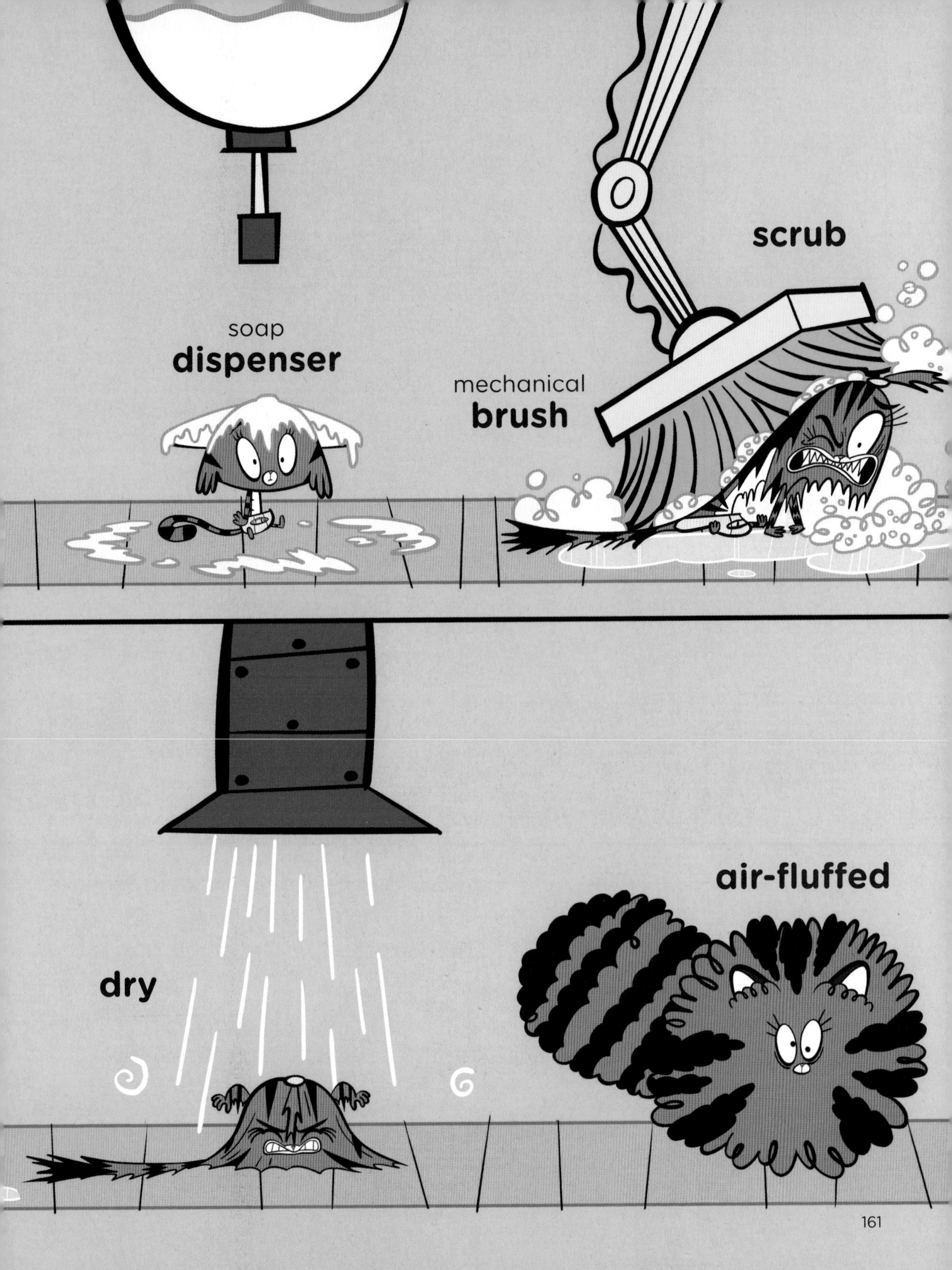
soap
dispenser
scrub
mechanical
brush
air-fluffed
dry

scalding **hot** **lukewarm**

adjust

move or change
something slightly

cold numbing glacial

BEAR HAIR CARE

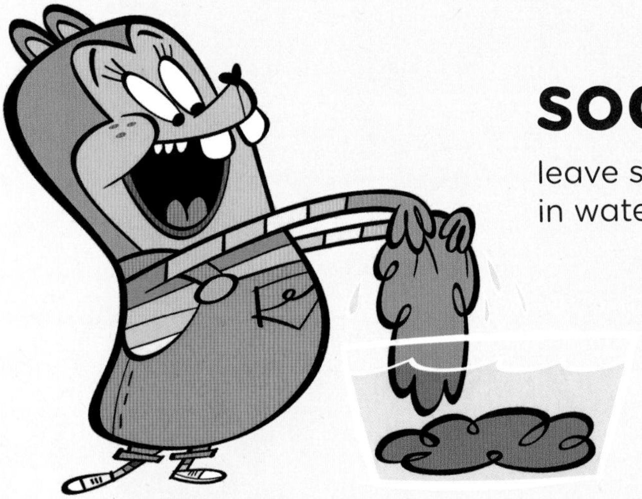

soak

leave something in water

shampoo

wash your hair with special hair soap

perm

pin curls

crew cut

ponytail

comb-over

bun

bob

braids

mohawk

Fix Up

polish
rub something to make it shinier

comb
get knots out of your hair with a comb

MRS wordsmith

brush

neaten your hair by running
a brush through it

apply lotion

rub cream into your skin

Dress Up

wide-brimmed
sun hat
skinny
jeans
frayed
shorts
baggy
sweatshirt
patterned
blouse
oversized
scarf
cashmere
gloves

get dressed

put clothes on

bowler
hat
pom-pom
hat
pleated
skirt
sharp
suit
snazzy
tie
warm
mittens
thick
socks

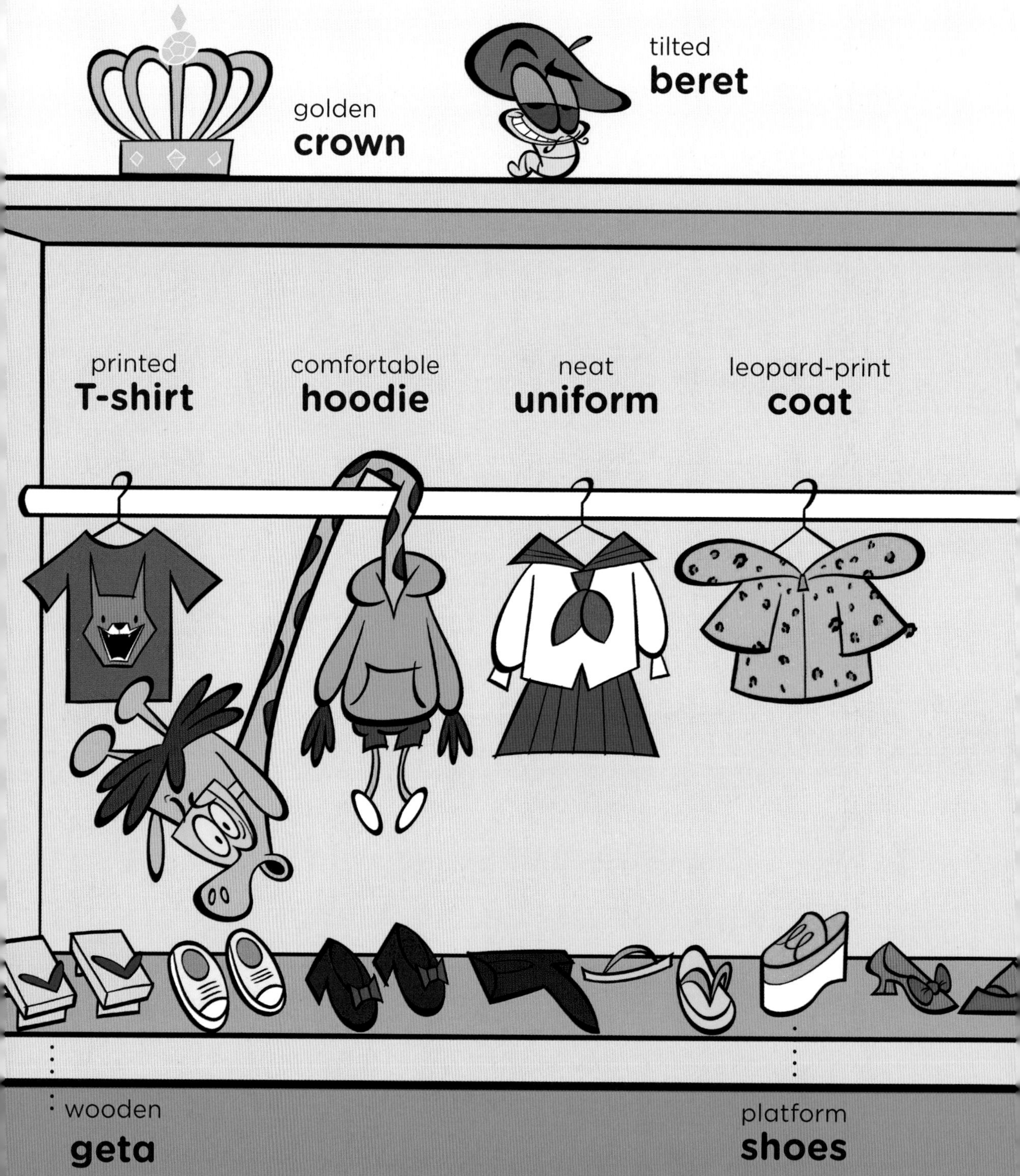
golden
crown
tilted
beret
printed
T-shirt
comfortable
hoodie
neat
uniform
leopard-print
coat
wooden
geta
platform
shoes

old-fashioned
top hat
baseball
cap
party
hat
matching
tracksuit
football
jersey
puffy
jacket
summer
dress
designer
sandals
cowboy
boots

LACE UP

classic
high-tops

understand

know how or why
something works

golden
low-tops

high-heel
high-tops

fluffy
high-tops

winged
high-tops

wheely
mid-tops

snakeskin
mid-tops

light-up
mid-tops

platform
low-tops

metallic
low-tops

moccasin
low-tops

imagine

use your mind to see the world completely differently

brave
knight

ferocious
dragon

STEALTH MODE

stealthy

trying not to be seen
or heard

telltale
clue

hide

cover something up
so no one sees it

inadequate
hiding place

seek

try to find

suspicious
footprints

conclusive
evidence

unusual
lamp

sloppy

careless and messy

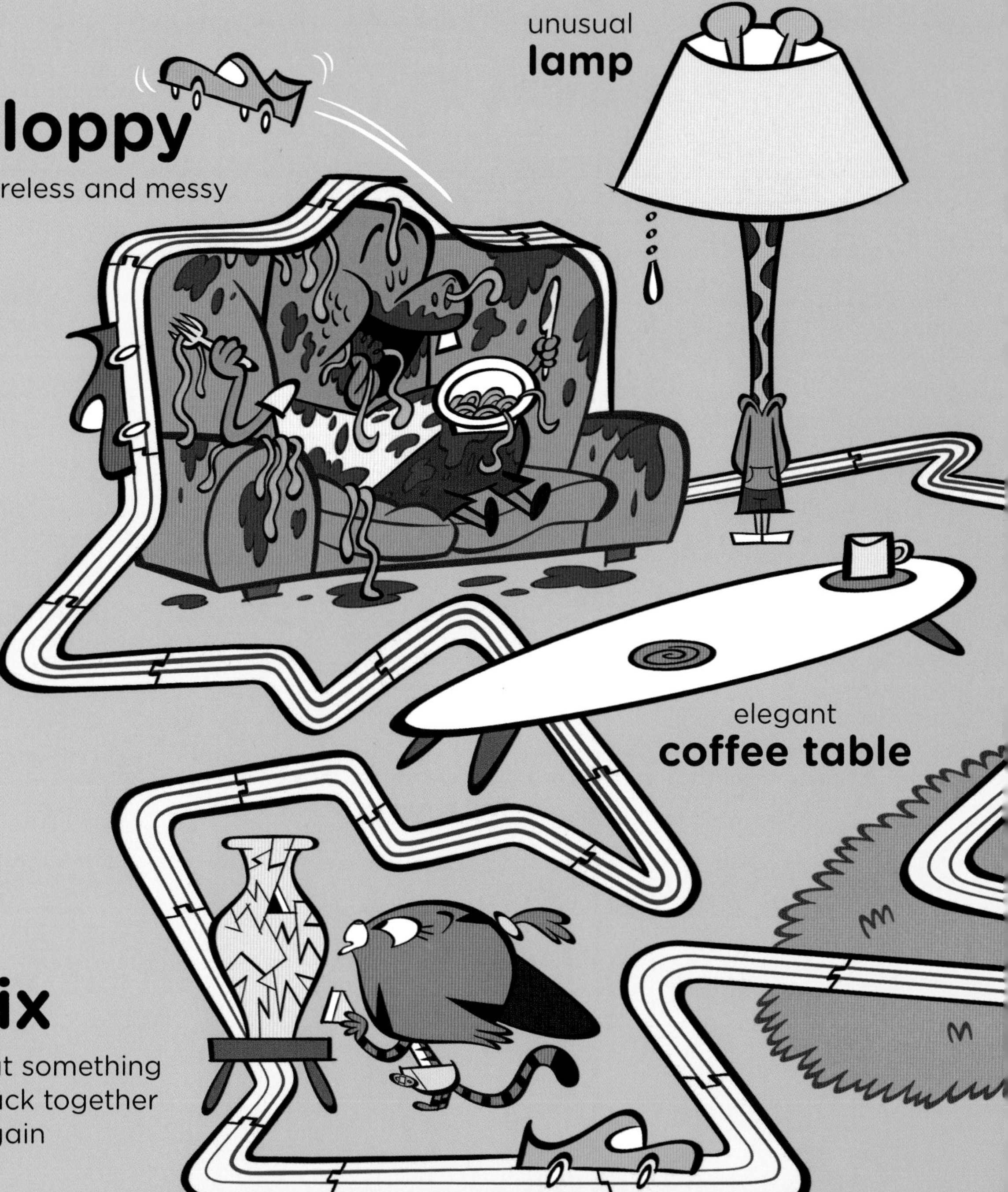

elegant
coffee table

fix

put something back together again

LIVING VROOOM
comfortable
armchair
epic
racetrack
shaggy
rug

DANGER ZONE

reckless

not caring about how dangerous something could be

risky

possibly causing something bad to happen

tempting
button

dangerous

not safe

electrical
cable

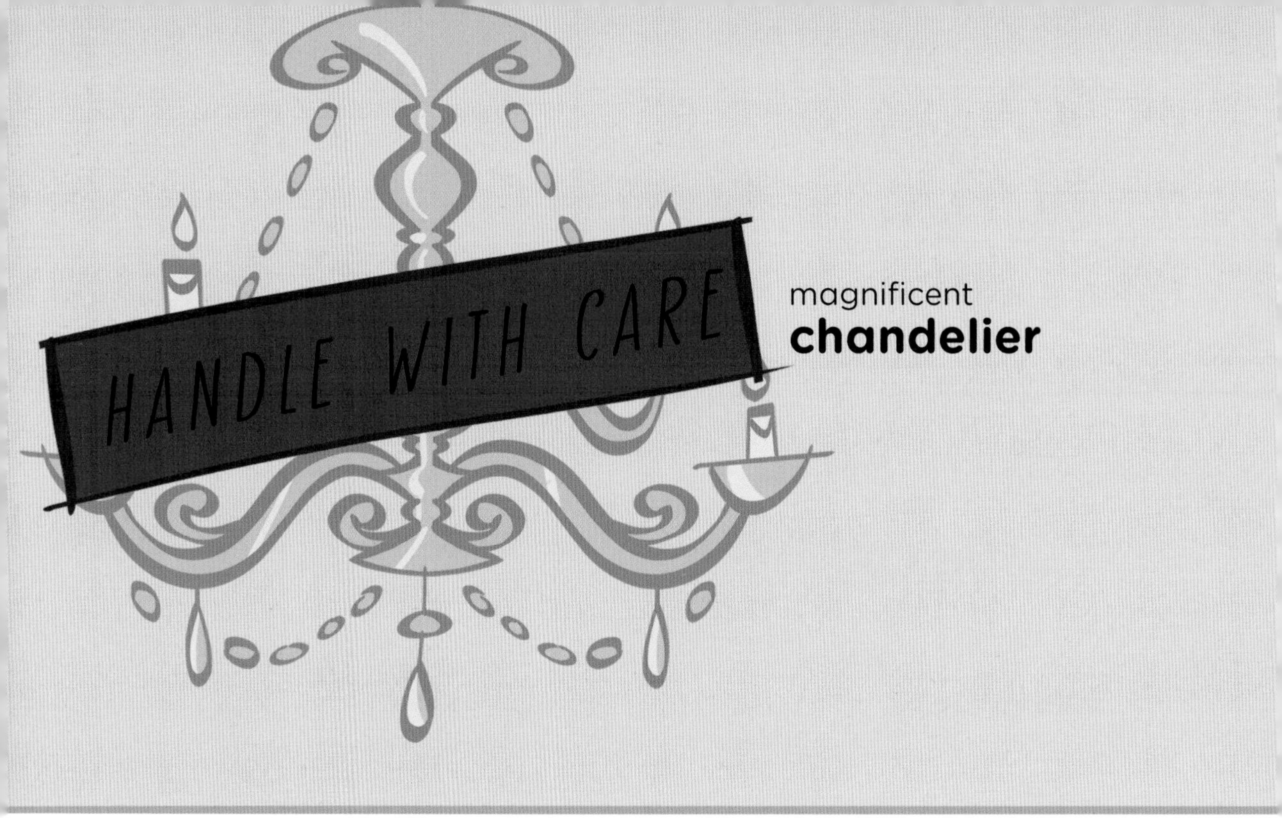
HANDLE WITH CARE
magnificent
chandelier

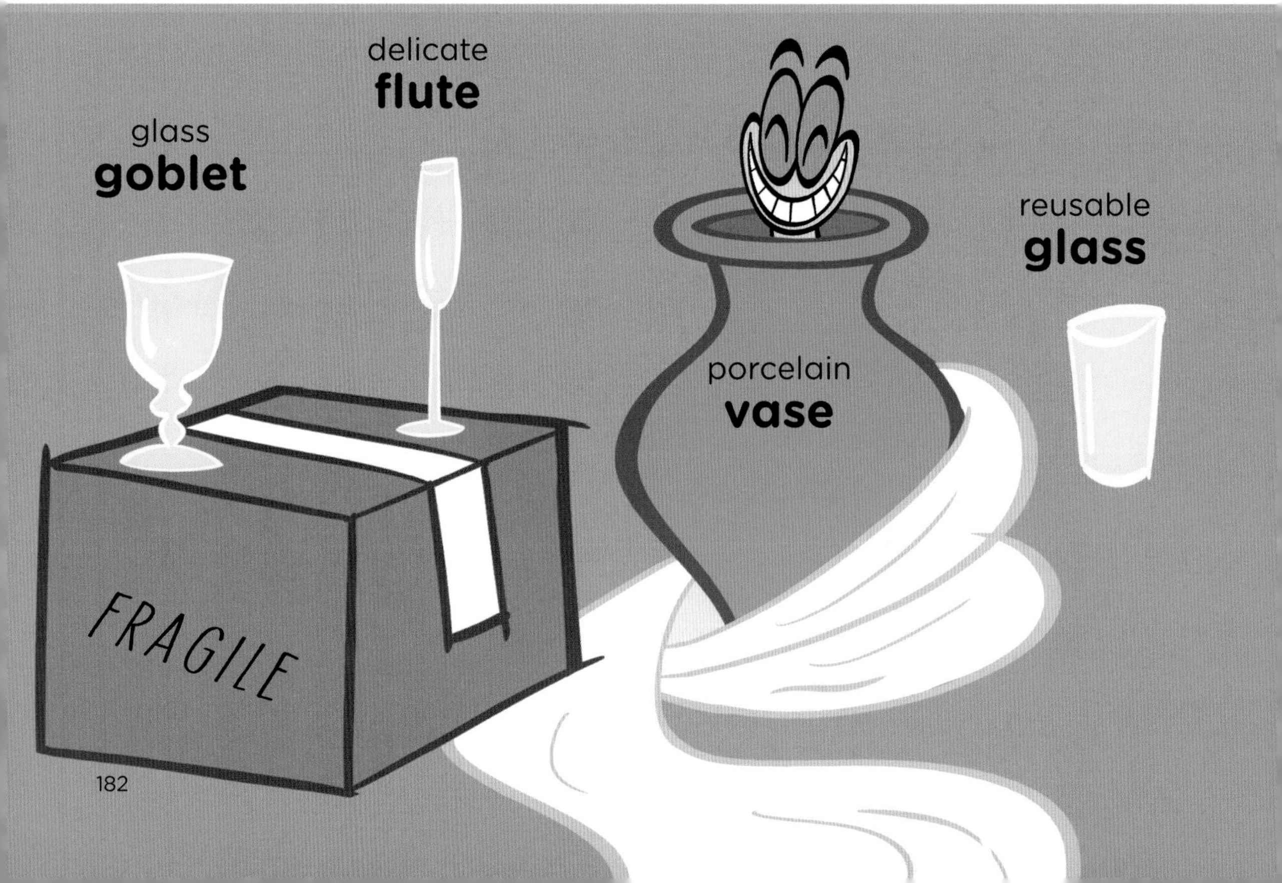
glass
goblet
delicate
flute
reusable
glass
porcelain
vase
FRAGILE

shatter

break into lots of little pieces

decorative
jug
sturdy
mug
vintage
teacup
cappuccino
cup

doodle

draw or scribble without thinking about it

CHILLING OUT

unwind

relax after being busy or worried

tranquil

calm and quiet

sleep

close your eyes and rest

moonlit
night
expansive
window
occupied
bed

wake up

stop sleeping

glorious
day

drawn
curtains

functional
bedside table

dream

things you see in your mind
when you're asleep

nightmare

a scary or upsetting dream

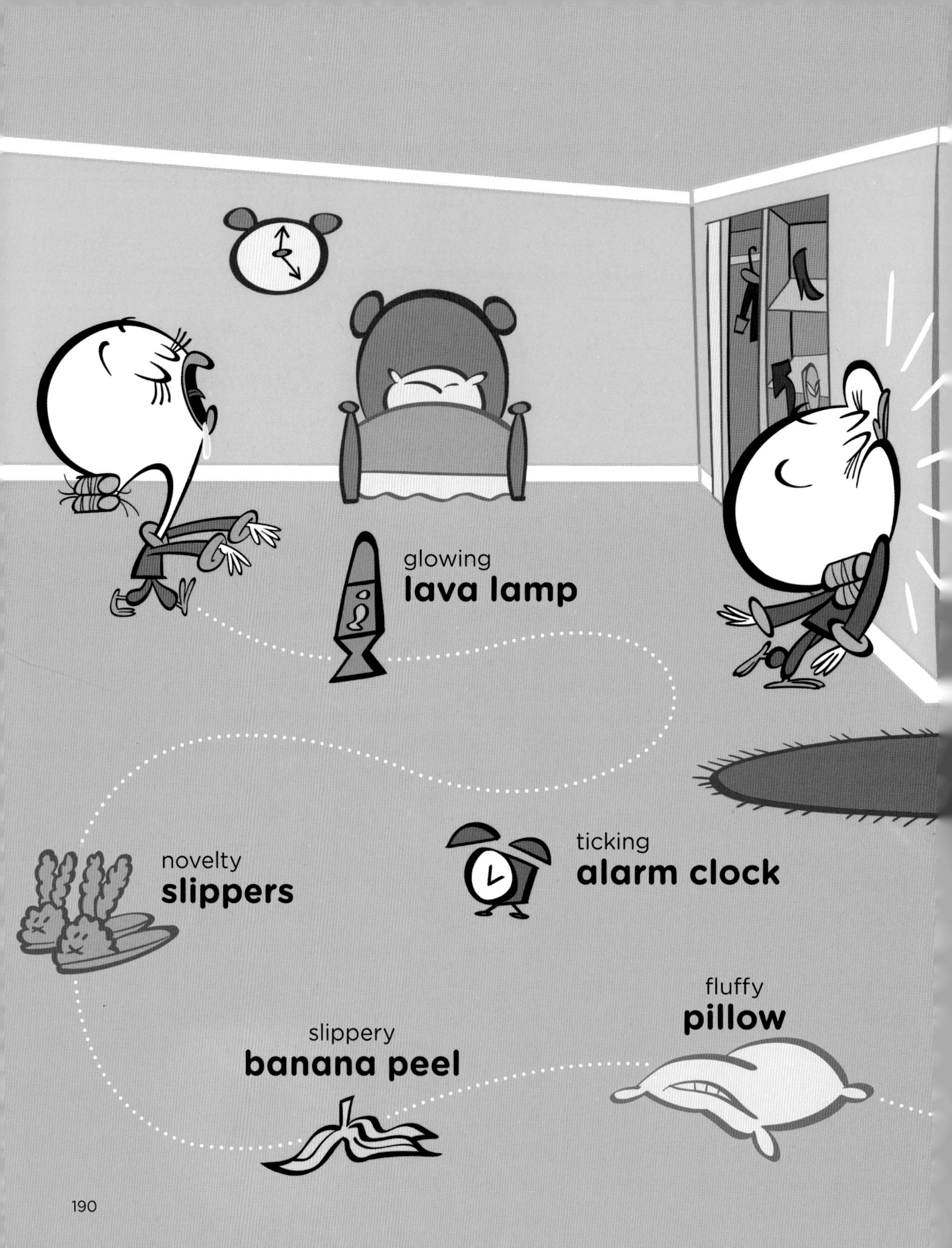
glowing
lava lamp
novelty
slippers
ticking
alarm clock
fluffy
pillow
slippery
banana peel

sleepwalk

get up and walk around
while asleep

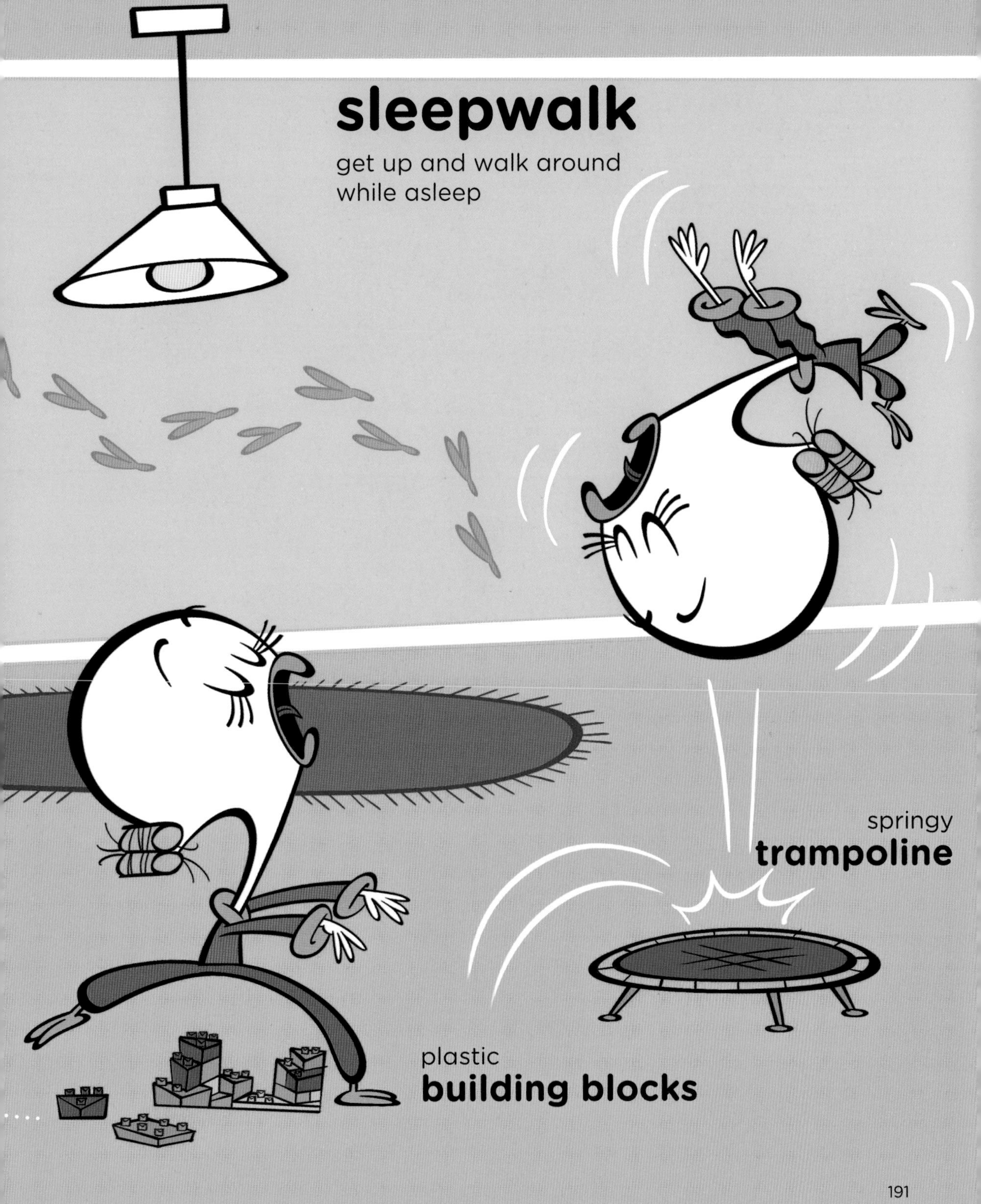
springy
trampoline
plastic
building blocks

WORDS FOR
OUTDOOR ADVENTURES

SCOOTOPIA

scooter **flip**
grind **rail**

safe

free from harm or danger

protective
helmet
steep
ramp

upset

sad or worried
about something

start
leap
sweat

tough

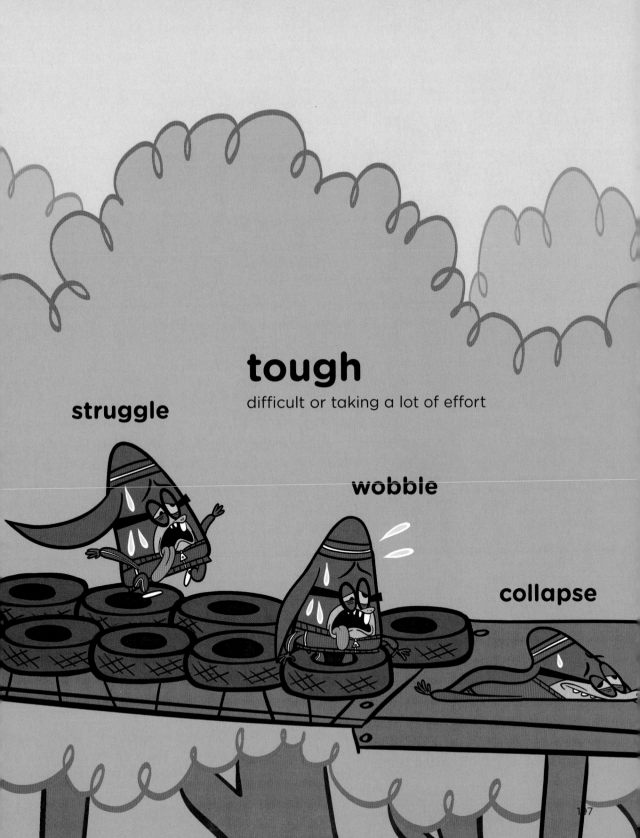

difficult or taking a lot of effort

struggle
wobble
collapse

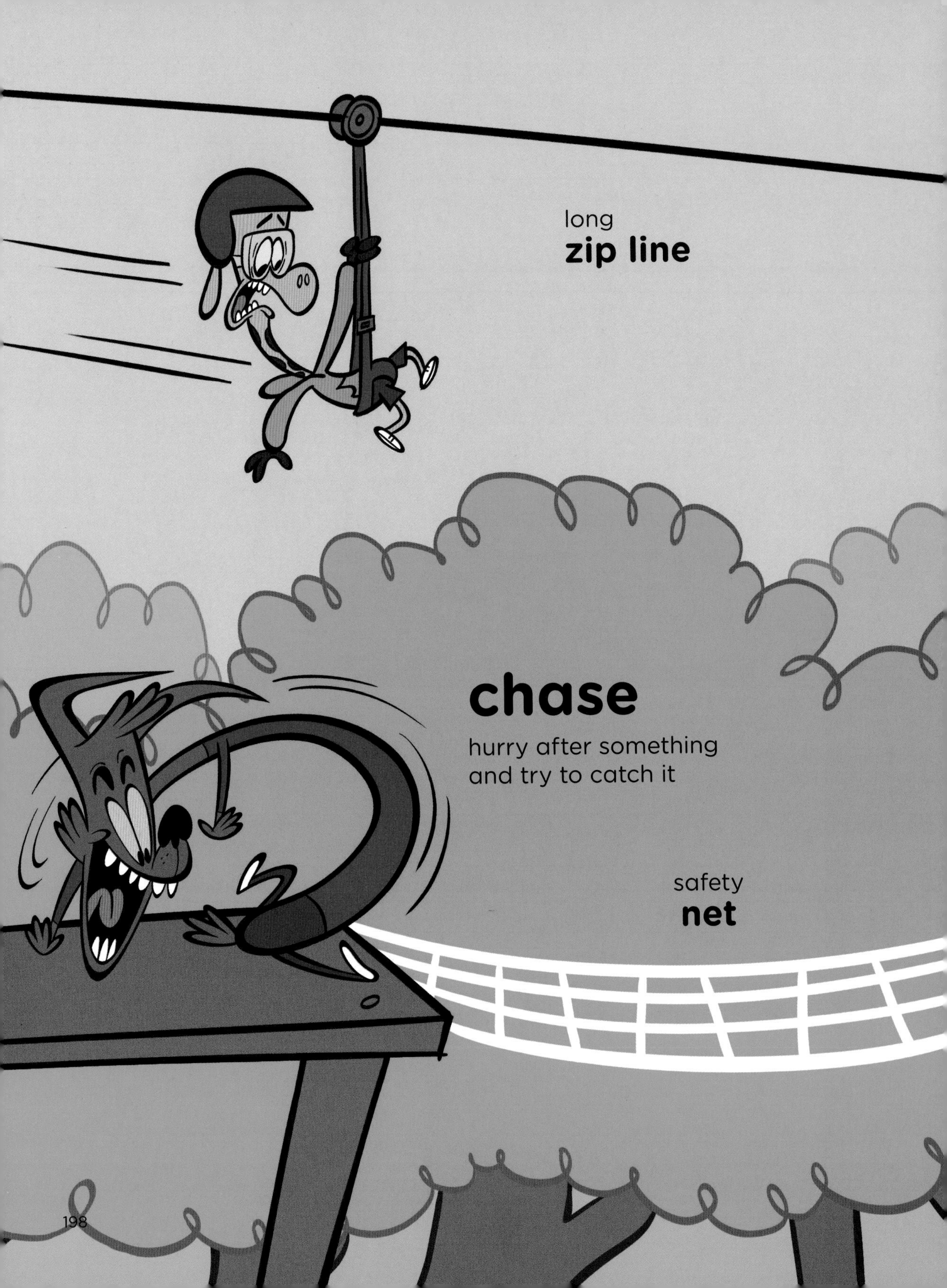

long
zip line

chase

hurry after something
and try to catch it

safety
net

frayed
rope

leafy
treetops

determined

not giving up

billowing
flags
challenge
something that is difficult
to do or finish

helpful
climbing holds
steep
climbing wall

reflect

think about things that
have happened

reflection

light and images that shine
back at you in the water

AT THE BEACH

naughty
crab

damp
beach towel

build

put things together to make something new

fragile
seashells

majestic
sandcastle

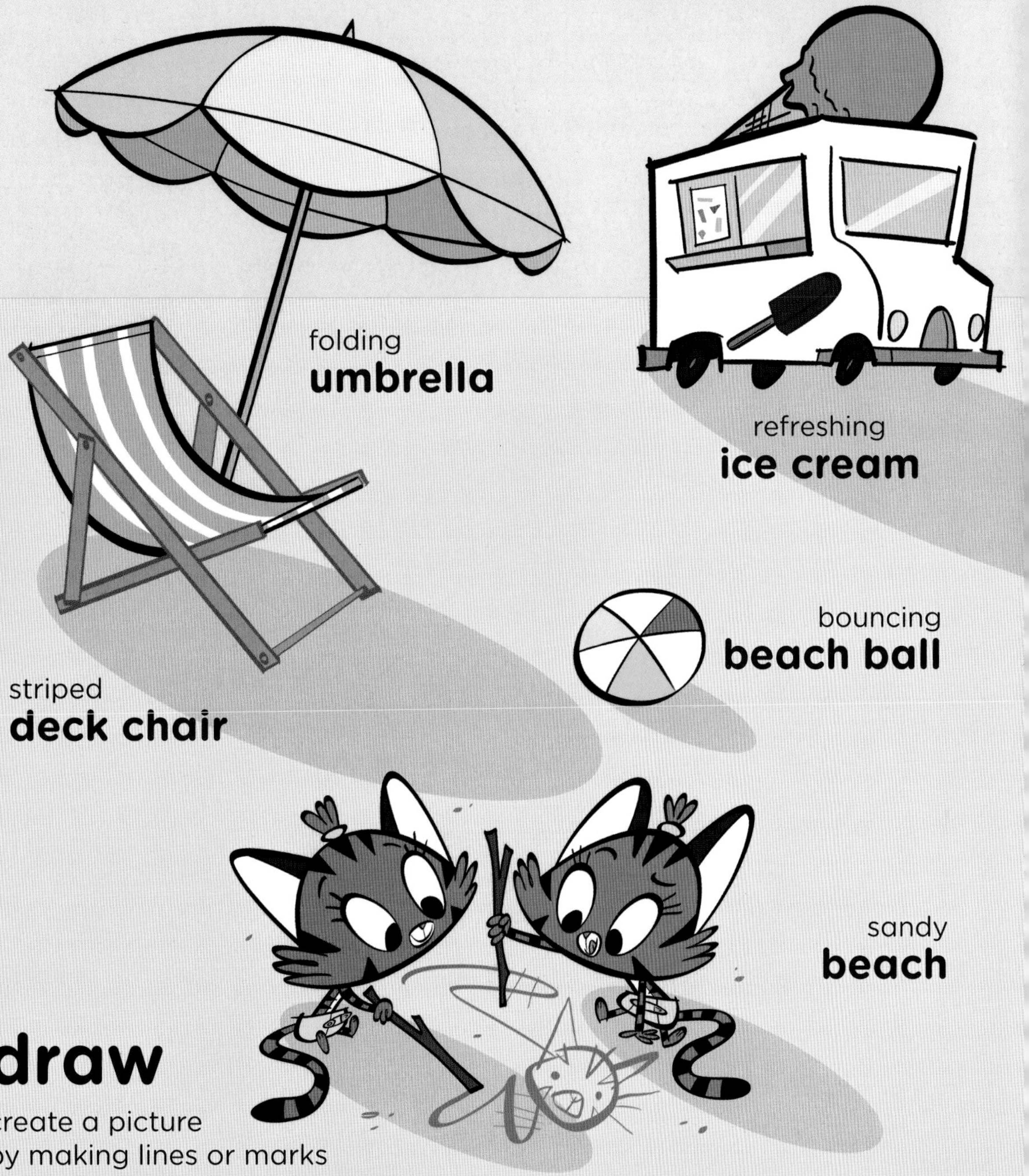

bountiful
ice cream truck

folding
umbrella

refreshing
ice cream

bouncing
beach ball

striped
deck chair

sandy
beach

draw

create a picture
by making lines or marks

squawking
seagull
golden
sand
polka dot
swimsuit
warning
sign
protective
suntan lotion
SPF
leaky
snorkel

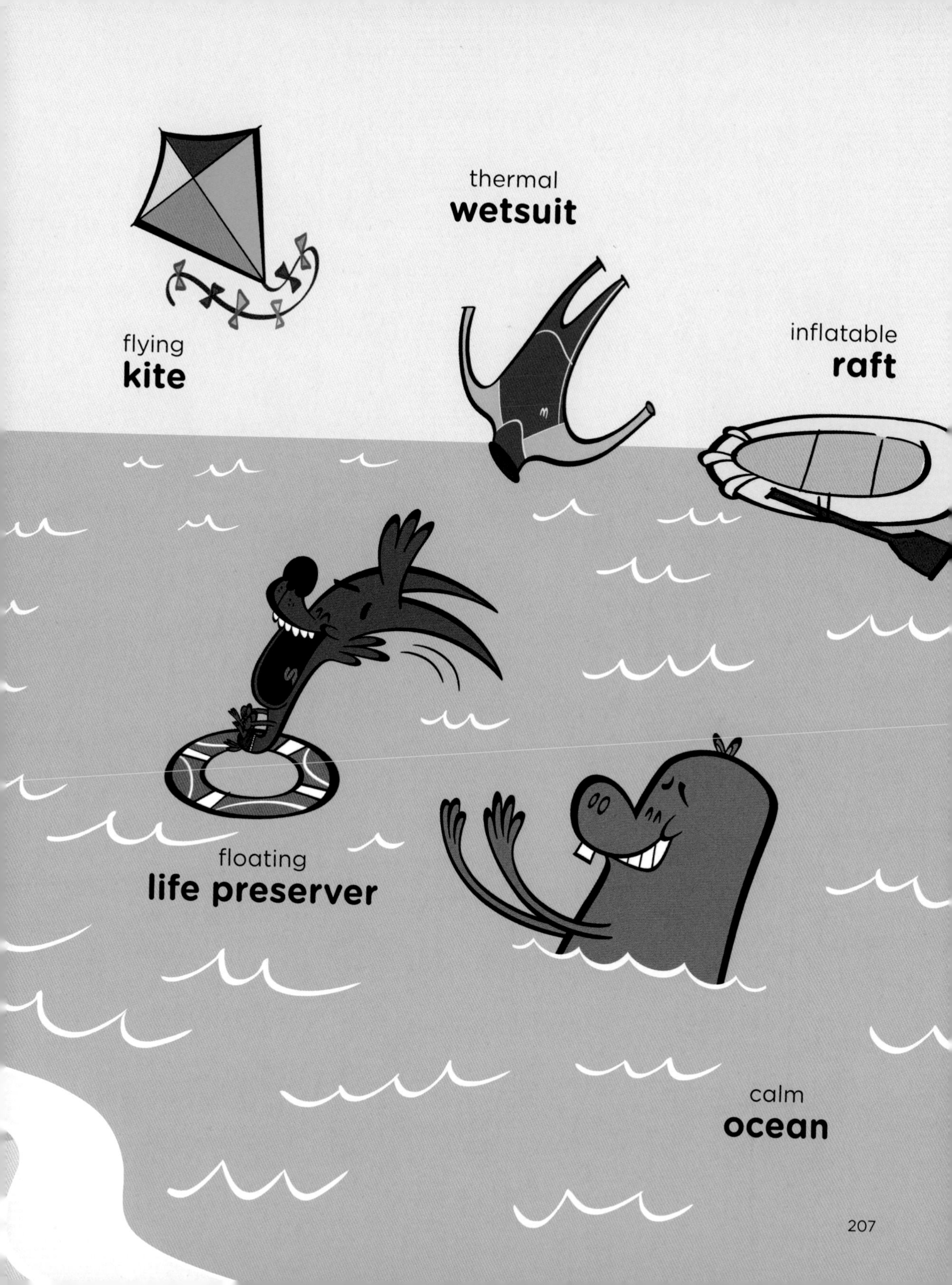
flying
kite
thermal
wetsuit
inflatable
raft
floating
life preserver
calm
ocean

curious

really wanting to find out more about something

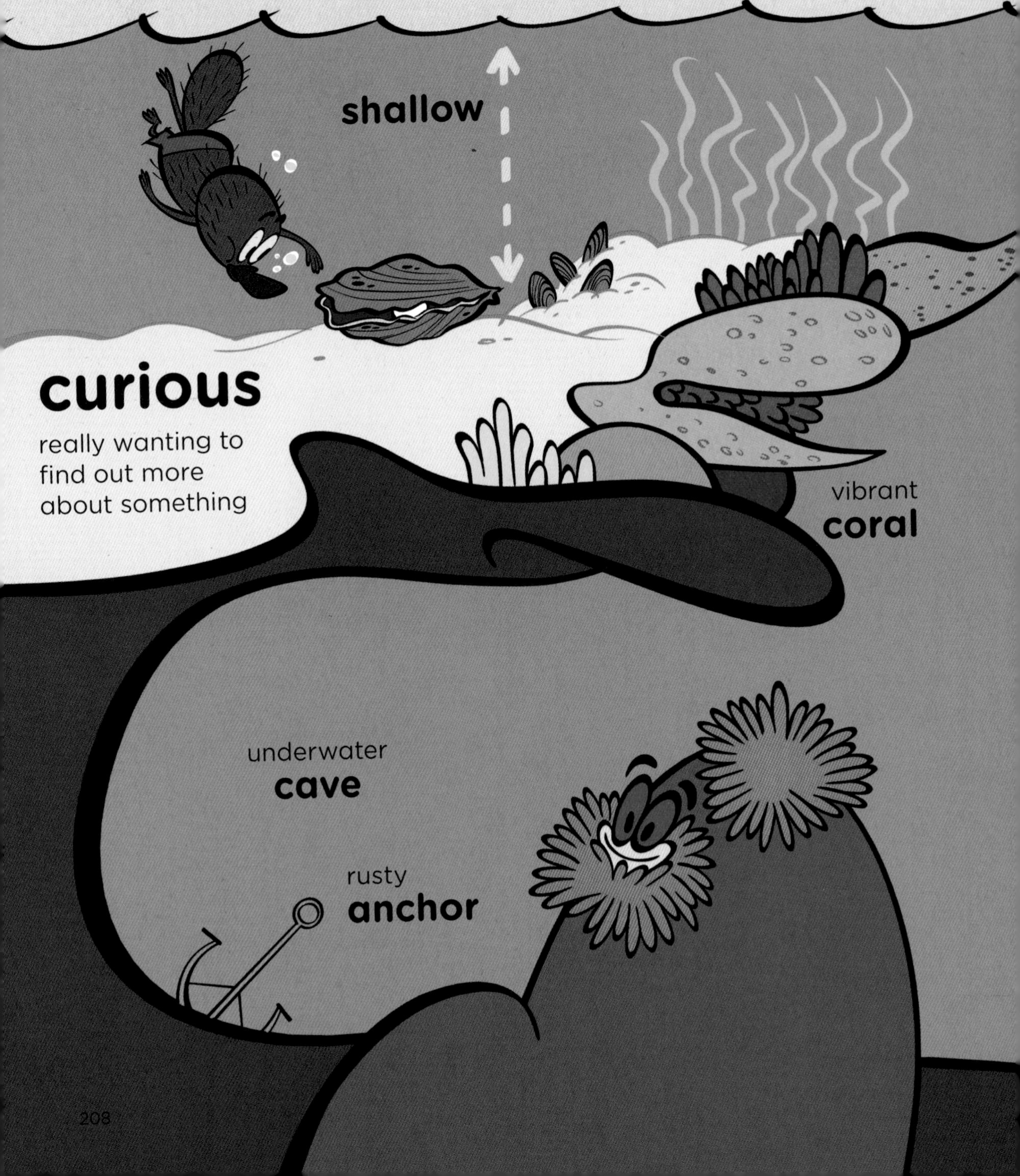
shallow
vibrant **coral**
underwater **cave**
rusty **anchor**

sneaky
periscope
DEEP BLUE
lurking
submarine
legendary
shipwreck
deep

inflatable
panda
inflatable
elephant
inflatable
parrot
Make a Splash!

shove

push someone
in a rude way

inflatable
giraffe
inflatable
lion
inflatable
shark
inflatable
flamingo

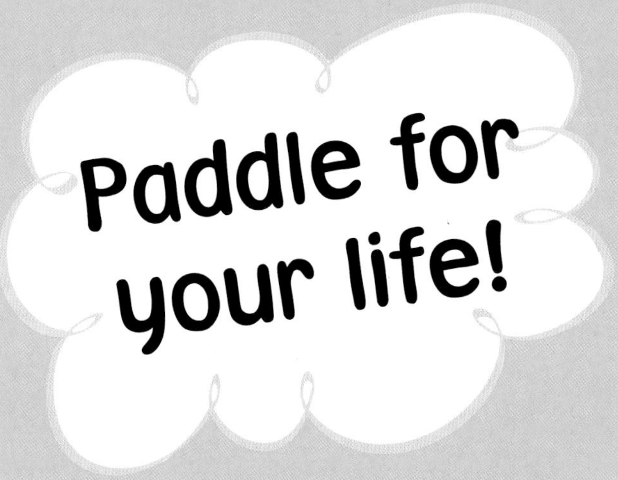
Paddle for your life!

anxious

worried about what might happen

inflatable
armbands

gulp

swallow a lot all at once

I can...

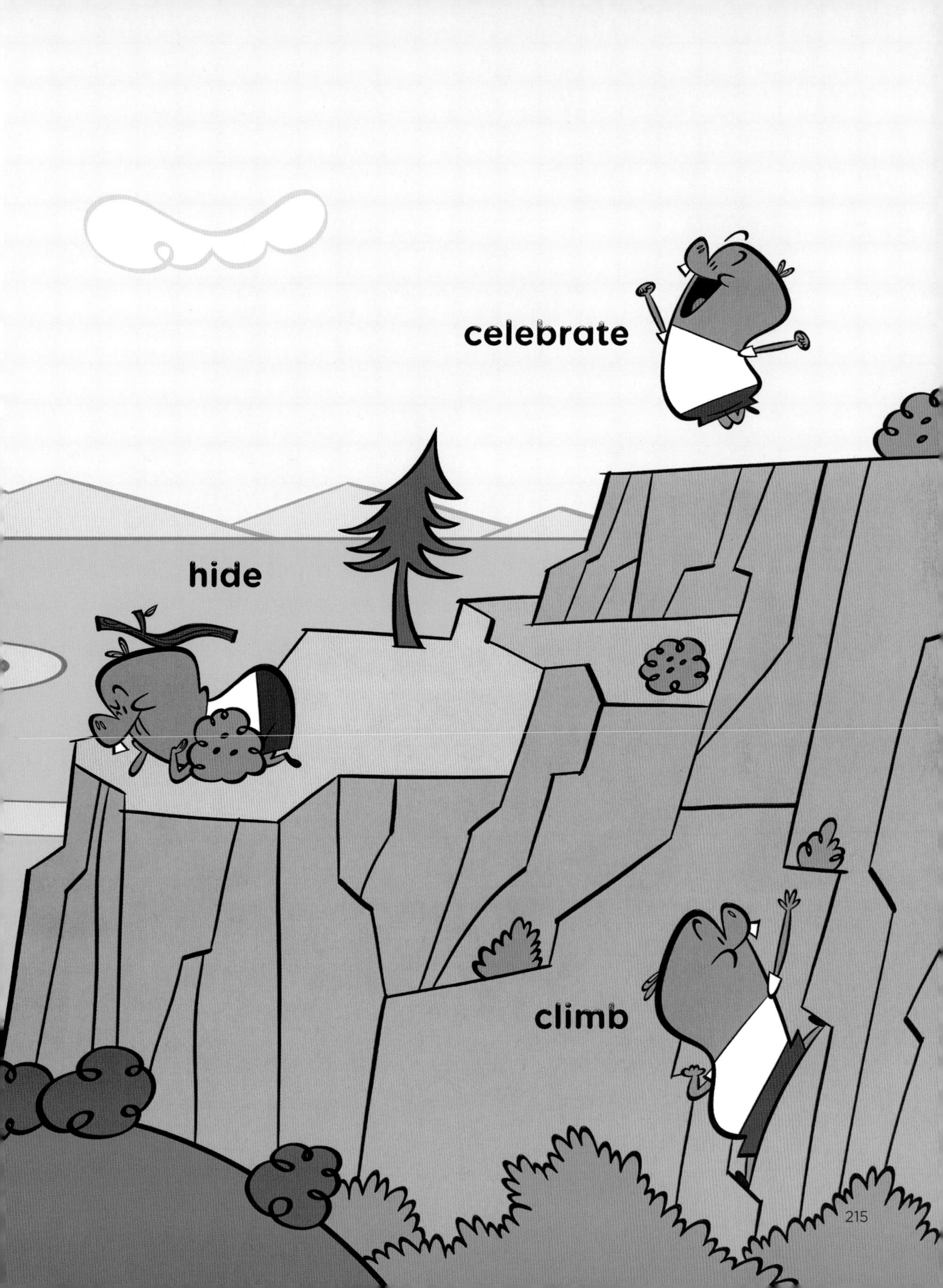
celebrate
hide
climb

extraordinary

incredible or very unusual

strawberry
cloud
elephant
cloud
bird
cloud
shark
cloud

race car
cloud
butterfly
cloud
rabbit
cloud

daydream

imagine nice things

spontaneous

happening without being planned

pine
trees
overhanging
cliff
shimmering
lake
evergreen
shrub
lush
grass

distant
mountains
carefree
not worried about anything
naked
platypus

FEEL THE BURN!

exercise

move your body a lot
to make it stronger

bouncy
exercise ball

persevere

keep going or carry on

MAX
BULK

concoct

make by mixing ingredients

heavy
dumbbell

compete

play against someone
or take part

THE NOT SO GREAT OUTDOORS
bare
branch
spooked
surprised by something that scares you
harmless
spider
dense
undergrowth

nocturnal **creatures**
huddle
crowd closely together with other people
crackling **campfire**

try

make an effort
to do something

fail

try to do something
and get it wrong

succeed

do well or achieve your goal

epic
fail

Good clean fun

muddy

covered in mud

muddy
puddle

muddy
laundry
muddy
splash

filthy

disgustingly dirty or yucky

half-eaten
pizza
vinyl
record
bulky
stereo
landline
phone

SO LAST GENERATION

sugary
cereal
broken
tricycle

awesome

amazing or incredible

WORD CARTOONS

adjust
p.163

challenge
p.200

dangerous
p.181

design
p.92

devour
p.147

drowsy
p.152

flush
p.155

gargle
p.51

gulp
p.213

hysterical
p.39

imagine
p.174

impressive
p.62

inspire
p.114

opposite
p.86

starving
p.143

tough
p.197

try
p.46

unroll
p.154

INDEX

A

3D printer, 93
accurate,
see **measuring cup**, 138
adhesive,
see **tape**, 96
adjust, 163
adventurous,
see **friend**, 23
air-fluffed, 161
airborne,
see **juggling clubs**, 117
alarm clock, 190
amazing, 83
ambitious,
see **blueprint**, 93
anchor, 208
angry, 35
animator, 109
anxious, 212
apple, 151
apply lotion, 167
April, 55
apron, 120
arm, 15
armbands, 213
armchair, 179
aromatic,
see **herbs**, 140
around, 81
ashen,
see **charcoal**, 127
August, 54
authentic,
see **taco**, 148
awake, 152
awesome, 230

B

baggy,
see **sweatshirt**, 168
banana, 151
banana peel, 190
bare,
see **branch**, 222
baseball,
see **cap**, 171
bashful, 42
basic bone broth, 52
bath, 158
bathtub, 159
beach, 205
beach ball, 205
beach towel, 204
beautiful,
see **crystal**, 94
bed, 186
bedside table, 187
beef, 140
behind, 79
beige, 127
belly, 15
beneath, 78
beret, 170
best, 129
see **friend**, 23
better, 128
between, 82
bib, 146
big, 70
billowing,
see **flags**, 200
bird,
see **cloud**, 216
birthday,
see **cake**, 43
birthday boy, 43
birthday girl, 44
black, 127
blame, 33
blouse, 168
blubber, 27
blue, 126, 127
blueberry, 150
blueprint, 93
bob, 165
body language, 113
bolts, 96
bone, 52
bone burger, 53
bone cone, 53
bones, 146
bones on toast, 53
bony,
see **knee**, 15
book, 112
boots, 171
boring,
see **beige**, 127
bouncing,
see **beach ball**, 205
bouncy,
see **exercise ball**, 220
bountiful,
see **ice cream truck**, 205
bowl, 142
bowler,
see **hat**, 169
braids, 165
branch, 222
brave,
see **knight**, 174
bread, 141
broccoli, 143
broken,
see **tricycle**, 229
brown, 127
see **spot**, 14
brush, 161, 167
bubble,
see **bath**, 158
build, 204
building blocks, 191
bulging,
see **belly**, 15
bulky,
see **stereo**, 228
bun, 95, 143, 165
burger, 94, 149
bushy,
see **tail**, 15
butter, 140
butterfly,
see **cloud**, 217
button, 181

C

cabbage, 140
cable, 181
cake, 43
calculator, 133
calm,
see **ocean**, 207
campfire, 223
candle, 43
candy apple,
see **red**, 126
canned,
see **tuna**, 141
canvas, 121
cap, 171
cappuccino,
see **cup**, 183
carefree, 219
carrot, 140
cashmere,
see **gloves**, 168
cast-iron,
see **griddle**, 144
catnapping, 153
cave, 208
celebrate, 215
celery, 140
ceramic,
see **mug**, 146
see **plate**, 139
cereal, 229
cereal box, 113
chair, 147, 205
chalk, 124
challenge, 200
chandelier, 182
charcoal, 127
chase, 198
cheerful, 34
chef, 145
chestnut,
see **brown**, 127
chicken, 140
chickenless bone bucket, 52
chopsticks, 139
circle, 68
circuit board, 95
classic,
see **burger**, 149
see **high-tops**, 172
clay, 124
clean,
see **cutting board**, 138
cliff, 218
climb, 215
climbing holds, 201
climbing wall, 201
cloud, 216, 217
clouds, 86, 87
clue, 176
coat, 170
cobalt,
see **blue**, 127
coconut, 151
coffee table, 178
cold, 163
collapse, 197
colossal, 70
comb, 166
comb-over, 165
comfort, 28
comfortable,
see **armchair**, 179
see **hoodie**, 170
compass, 133
compete, 221
complex,
see **circuit board**, 95
computer, 101
concept artist, 107
conclusive,
see **evidence**, 177
concoct, 221
confused, 35
coral, 208
cowboy, 95
see **boots**, 171
crab, 204
cracked,
see **pepper**, 141
crackling,
see **campfire**, 223
crawl, 130
crayons, 125
creamy,
see **butter**, 140
create, 93
creatures, 223
crew cut, 165
crown, 170
crunchy,
see **celery**, 140
crusty,
see **bread**, 141
cry, 26
crystal, 94
cup, 138, 183
curious, 208
curry powder, 141
curtains, 187
cutting board, 138
cutting-edge,
see **hoverboard**, 50

D

damp,
see **beach towel**, 204
dangerous, 181
dangling,
see **piñata**, 45
day, 187
daydream, 217
December, 55
deck chair, 205
decorative,
see **jug**, 183
deep, 209
delicate,
see **flute**, 182
dense,
see **undergrowth**, 222
design, 92
designer,
see **sandals**, 171
desperate, 156

determined, 199
devour, 147
difficult, 116
dining table, 147
dinosaur,
 see puzzle, 116
disco ball, 43
dispenser, 161
distant,
 see mountains, 219
dog, 59
doodle, 184
doughnut, 94
 see scooter, 99
dragon, 59, 175
draw, 205
drawn,
 see curtains, 187
dream, 188
dress, 171
drill, 97
driverless,
 see scooter, 99
drone, 97
drowsy, 152
dry, 161
dumbbell, 221
dumplings, 148

E

eager, 144
ear, 14
earphones, 132
easel, 121
eat, 147
ecstatic, 158
egg, 95
eggshell,
 see white, 126
eighty, 67
electric,
 see drill, 97
 see purple, 126
electrical,
 see cable, 181
elegant,
 see chopsticks, 139
 see coffee table, 178
elephant, 210
 see cloud, 216
elongated,
 see nose, 14
email, 113
emerald,
 see green, 126
empower, 135
empty,
 see bowl, 142
 see roll, 157
enormous, 70
 see present, 42
enthusiastic, 100
epic,
 see race track, 179
epic fail, 225
evergreen,
 see shrub, 218
evidence, 177
excited, 100
exclude, 37
exercise, 220
exercise ball, 220
expansive,
 see window, 186
expensive,
 see phone, 100
 see saffron, 141
extraordinary, 216
extravagant,
 see lobster, 94
eye, 14

F

fail, 224, 225
fall (season), 57
family,
 see friend, 23
February, 54
ferocious,
 see dragon, 175
festive,
 see bunting, 45
fierce,
 see tiger, 95
fiery,
 see hot sauce, 141
fifteen, 64
 see saffron,141
fifty, 66
filthy, 228
finger, 15
five, 63
 see shrimp, 140
fix, 178
flags, 45, 200
flamingo, 211
flickering,
 see candle, 43
flip, 194
floating,
 see life buoy, 207
floppy,
 see ear, 14
flour, 141
fluffy,
 see high-tops, 173
 see pillow, 190
 see quinoa, 141
flush, 155
flustered, 157
flute, 182
focus, 135
folded,
 see napkin, 139
folding,
 see umbrella, 205
football,
 see jersey, 171
footlong,
 see hot dog, 148
footprints, 177
forgive, 33
fork, 139
forty, 66
fragile,
 see seashells, 204

frayed,
see **rope,** 199
see **shorts,** 168
free-range,
see **chicken,** 140
free-standing,
see **bathtub,** 159
fresh,
see **cabbage,** 140
Friday, 52
fried,
see **egg,** 95
friend, 23
friends, 22
friendship,
see **friendship bracelet,** 22
friendship bracelet, 22
frown, 40
frying pan, 145
functional,
see **bedside table,** 187
furious, 116
fuzzy,
see **kiwi,** 150

G

game designer, 102
game tester, 108
gaping,
see **mouth,** 15
gargle, 51
garlic, 141
get dressed, 169
geta, 170
gigantic, 70
ginger, 140
giraffe, 211
glacial, 163
glass, 182
see **goblet,** 182
glazed,
see **doughnut,** 94
glitter, 125
gloomy,
see **clouds,** 86
glorious,
see **day,** 187
gloves, 168
glowing,
see **lava lamp,** 190
glue, 124
glum, 35
goat, 58
goblet, 182
golden,
see **crown,** 170
see **low-tops,** 172
see **sand,** 206
see **sunshine,** 87
good, 128
goofy, 34
gourmet,
see **burger,** 94
grape, 151
grass, 218
green, 126
griddle, 144
grind,
see **rail,** 194
gulp, 213

H

hair, 14
half-eaten,
see **pizza,** 228
ham, 140
hammer, 96
hand, 15
hand-painted,
see **mural,** 125
hand-picked,
see **grape,** 151
hand-rolled,
see **sushi,** 149
handheld,
see **whisk,** 139
handmade,
see **pasta,** 141
handy,
see **calculator,** 133
happy, 34
harmless,
see **spider,** 222
hat, 169, 171
head, 14
headset, 101
healthy,
see **salad,** 149
heatproof,
see **spatula,** 138
heavy,
see **dumbbell,** 221
see **lid,** 145
see **raindrops,** 86
see **wrench,** 96
heavy dumbbell, 221
helmet, 96, 195
helpful,
see **climbing holds,** 201
hemp,
see **bib,** 146
herbs, 140
hexagon, 69
hide, 176, 215
hiding place, 176
high, 72
high-heel,
see **high-tops,** 173
high-performance,
see **motorcycle,** 98
high-tops, 172, 173
hoodie, 170
horse, 58
hot, 162
hot dog, 148
hot sauce, 141
hover,
see **scooter,** 99
hoverboard, 50, 99
hovering,
see **drone,** 97
howling, 39
huddle, 223
huge, 71
humble,
see **potato,** 141

hunched,
see **shoulder,** 15
hungry, 142
hysterical, 39

I

I can, 214
ice cream, 205
ice cream van, 205
imagine, 174
impressive, 62
in, 59, 78
in front of, 79
inadequate,
see **hiding place,** 176
include, 36
incredible,
see **3D printer,** 93
index,
see **finger,** 15
inflatable,
see **armbands,** 213
see **elephant,** 210
see **flamingo,** 211
see **giraffe,** 211
see **lion,** 211
see **panda,** 210
see **parrot,** 210
see **raft,** 207
see **shark,** 211
influence, 134
inspire, 114
insulted, 121
intense, 101
invent, 96

J

jacket, 171
jagged,
see **saw,** 97
January, 54
jeans, 168
jersey, 171
jet,
see **black,** 127
jug, 183
juggling clubs, 117
juicy,
see **shrimp,** 140
July, 54
June, 55

K

kebab, 148
kite, 207
kiwi, 150
knee, 15
knife, 138
knight, 174

L

lake, 218
lamp, 178
landline,
see **phone,** 228
laptop, 100
large,
see **onion,** 140
latest,
see **laptop,** 100
lather, 160
laughing, 34, 38
laundry, 227
lava lamp, 190
leafy,
see **treetops,** 199
leaky,
see **snorkel,** 206
leap, 196
leftover,
see **ham,** 140
leftovers, 146
leg, 15
legendary,
see **shipwreck,** 209
lemon, 151
see **yellow,** 126
leopard print,
see **coat,** 170
lid, 145
life preserver, 207
light-speed,
see **space racer,** 94
light-up,
see **mid-tops,** 173
lightning, 86
lion, 211
lobster, 94
lock, 156
lofty, 73
long,
see **zip line,** 198
loose,
see **bolts,** 96
love, 16
low-tops, 172, 173
lucky,
see **birthday boy,** 43
see **birthday girl,** 44
lukewarm, 162
lurking,
see **submarine,** 209
luscious,
see **strawberry,** 150
lush,
see **grass,** 218

M

magnificent,
see **chandelier,** 182
majestic,
see **sandcastle,** 204
manual,
see **toothbrush,** 51
map, 113
March, 54
marshmallow, 81
massive, 71
masterpiece, 123
matching,
see **tracksuit,** 171

May, 55
measuring,
see tape, 97
measuring cup, 138
mechanical,
see brush, 161
metal,
see spatula, 139
metallic,
see spray paint, 125
see low-tops, 173
mid-tops, 173
milk,
see scooter, 98
millennial,
see pink, 126
minds, 113
minty,
see toothpaste, 51
minuscule, 70
minutes, 51
mischievous, 32
miserable, 159
mittens, 169
moccasin,
see low-tops, 173
mohawk, 165
moist,
see clay, 124
Monday, 52
monkey, 58
moonlit,
see night, 186
motorcycle, 98
mountains, 219
mouth, 15
muddled, 85
muddy, 226
see laundry, 227
see puddle, 226
see splash, 227
mug, 146, 183
mural, 125
music-loving,
see robot, 97

N

naked,
see platypus, 219
napkin, 139
naughty,
see crab, 204
neat, 138
see uniform, 170
neck, 14
need, 92
net, 198
new,
see friend, 23
newspaper, 113
next to, 79
nibble, 146
night, 186
nightmare, 189
ninety, 67
nocturnal,
see creatures, 223
nonconformist, 20
nonstick,
see skillet, 145
noodles, 148
nose, 14
novel, 112
novelty,
see slippers, 190
November, 55
numbing, 163
nuts, 96

O

obsessed, 101
occupied,
see bed, 186
ocean, 207
octagon, 69
October, 55
old,
see friend, 23
old-fashioned,
see top hat, 47
olive oil, 141
on, 78
one hundred, 67
onion, 140
opposite, 86
orange, 127, 151
organic,
see beef, 140
see carrot, 140
see pear, 151
ossicone, 14
over, 80
overflowing,
see toilet, 155
overhanging,
see cliff, 218
overripe,
see banana, 151
oversized,
see scarf, 168
ox, 58

P

paint, 120
paintbrush, 124
pancake, 144
panda, 210
parrot, 210
party,
see hat, 171
passion, 123
pasta, 141
patterned,
see blouse, 168
pear, 151
pencil case, 132
pentagon, 69
pepper, 141
peppery,
see radish, 140
periscope, 209
perm, 165
persevere, 220
phone, 100, 228
picture, 124

pies, 147
pig, 59
pillow, 190
pin curls, 165
piñata, 45
pine,
see **trees**, 218
pink, 127
pipes, 155
pity, 30
pizza, 148, 228
plastic,
see **building blocks**, 191
see **pipes**, 155
plate, 139
platform,
see **low-tops**, 173
see **shoes**, 170
platypus, 219
playful, 34
playing cards, 117
pleated,
see **skirt**, 169
plump,
see **blueberry**, 150
polish, 166
polite, 25
polka dot,
see **swimsuit**, 206
pom-pom,
see **hat**, 169
pomegranate,
see **pink**, 127
ponytail, 165
porcelain,
see **vase**, 182
portable,
see **potty**, 157
potato, 141
potato peeler, 139
potty, 157
pout, 40
power,
see **shower**, 159
powerful,
see **computer**, 101
see **hammer**, 96
practice, 129
present, 42
printed,
see **T-shirt**, 170
problem, 118
producer, 103
programmer, 108
propeller,
see **helmet**, 96
protective,
see **helmet**, 195
puddle, 226
puffy,
see **jacket**, 171
pungent,
see **garlic**, 141
pure,
see **olive oil**, 141
purple, 126
puzzle, 116

Q

quilted,
see **toilet paper**, 154
quinoa, 141

R

rabbit, 59
see **cloud**, 217
race car,
see **cloud**, 217
racetrack, 179
radish, 140
raft, 207
rail, 194
raindrops, 86
rainfall,
see **shower head**, 160
ramp, 195
rat, 58
raw,
see **ginger**, 140
read, 112
see **body language**, 113
see **book**, 112
see **cereal box**, 113
see **email**, 113
see **map**, 113
see **minds**, 113
see **newspaper**, 113
see **novel**, 112
reckless, 180
record, 228
rectangle, 69
red, 126
red-hot,
see **stove**, 145
reflect, 202
reflection, 202
refreshing,
see **ice cream**, 205
see **watermelon**, 151
regret, 64
reject, 143
relate, 31
relief, 157
researcher, 105
respect, 24
reusable,
see **glass**, 182
rhombus, 69
right way up, 85
rinse, 160
risky, 181
robot, 97
robotic,
see **chef**, 145
roll, 157
rooster, 59
rope, 199
rosy,
see **apple**, 151
rotating,
see **disco ball**, 43
rough,
see **sketch**, 92
rug, 179
run, 131

rusty,
see **anchor,** 208

S

sad, 35
safe, 194
safety,
see **net,** 198
saffron, 141
salad, 149
salt, 141
sand, 206
sandals, 171
sandcastle, 204
sandy,
see **beach,** 205
Saturday, 53
saucepan, 145
saw, 97
scalding, 162
scarf, 168
scattered,
see **playing cards,** 117
scissors, 96
scooter, 98, 99
see **flip,** 194
scorching,
see **sun,** 87
scowl, 41
screwdrivers, 97
scribbled,
see **picture,** 124
scrub, 161
scrumptious,
see **pies,** 147
sculpt, 122
sea,
see **salt,** 141
seagull, 206
seashells, 204
seconds, 50
secure,
see **lock,** 156
seek, 177
self-balancing,
see **hoverboard,** 99
September, 54
serving,
see **spoon,** 139
sesame seed,
see **bun,** 143
seventy, 67
shaggy,
see **rug,** 179
shallow, 208
shampoo, 164
share, 74
shark, 211
see **cloud,** 216
sharp,
see **knife,** 138
see **scissors,** 96
see **suit,** 169
see **tooth,** 14
shatter, 183
shimmering,
see **lake,** 218
shipwreck, 209
shoes, 170
shortcut, 118
shorts, 168
shoulder, 15
shove, 211
shower, 160
shower head, 159
shriek, 149
shrimp, 140
shrub, 218
sign, 206
silken,
see **tofu,** 140
silver,
see **fork,** 139
simple,
see **screwdriver,** 97
sixty, 66
sizzling,
see **frying pan,** 145
sketch, 92
skillet, 145
skinny,
see **jeans,** 168
skip, 130
skirt, 169
sky,
see **blue,** 126
sleep, 186
sleepwalk, 191
slender,
see **neck,** 14
slippers, 190
slippery,
see **banana peel,** 190
sloppy, 178
small, 70
snake, 59
snakeskin,
see **mid-tops,** 173
snazzy,
see **tie,** 169
sneaky,
see **periscope,** 209
snorkel, 206
soak, 164
soap,
see **dispenser,** 161
soaring, 72
see **pancake,** 144
sob, 26
socks, 169
solution, 119
sour,
see **lemon,** 151
space racer, 94
spatula, 138, 139
spectacular,
see **lightning,** 86
spicy,
see **curry powder,** 141
spider, 222
spiky,
see **compass,** 133
spilled,
see **glitter,** 125
splash, 227
spontaneous, 218
spooked, 222

spoon, 138, 139
spot, 14
spotless,
see **apron**, 120
spray paint, 125
spring, 56
springy,
see **trampoline**, 191
square, 68
squawking,
see **seagull**, 206
squeal, 44
stainless-steel,
see **saucepan**, 145
star, 69
start, 196
starving, 143
steady,
see **hand**, 15
stealthy, 176
steamed,
see **broccoli**, 143
see **dumplings**, 148
steel,
see **nuts**, 96
steep,
see **ramp**, 195
stereo, 228
sticky,
see **noodles**, 148
stove, 145
strawberry, 150
see **cloud**, 216
striped,
see **deck chair**, 205
strong,
see **vinegar**, 141
struggle, 197
stubby,
see **thumb**, 15
sturdy,
see **chair**, 147
see **mug**, 183
stylish,
see **dining table**, 147
submarine, 209
succeed, 225
succulent,
see **kebab**, 148
sugary,
see **cereal**, 229
suit, 169
sulk, 41
summer, 56
see **dress**, 171
sun, 87, 206
sun hat, 168
Sunday, 53
sunshine, 87
suntan lotion, 206
supersize bone, 53
sushi, 149
suspicious,
see **footprints**, 177
swaggering,
see **cowboy**, 95
sweat, 196
sweatshirt, 168
sweet potato, 140
swimsuit, 206
sympathetic, 29

T

T-shirt, 170
tablet, 100
taco, 148
tail, 15
tangerine,
see **orange**, 127
tangled,
see **earphones**, 132
tangy,
see **orange**, 151
tape, 96, 97
tasty,
see **bones**, 146
taut,
see **canvas**, 121
teacup, 183
telltale,
see **clue**, 176
tempting,
see **button**, 181
ten,
see **regret** 63, 66
thermal,
see **wetsuit**, 207
thick,
see **paintbrush**, 124
see **socks**, 169
think, 69
thirty, 66
through, 83
thumb, 15
Thursday, 52
ticking,
see **alarm clock**, 190
tie, 169
tiger, 58, 95
tilted,
see **beret**, 170
toe, 15
tofu, 140
toilet, 155
see **scooter**, 99
toilet paper, 154
tooth, 14
toothbrush, 51
toothpaste, 51
top hat, 171
touchscreen,
see **tablet**, 100
tough, 197
towering, 73
tracksuit, 171
trampoline, 191
tranquil, 185
trees, 218
treetops, 199
triangle, 68
tricky, 117
tricycle, 229
tropical,
see **coconut**, 151
see **turquoise**, 127
true,
see **friend**, 23
try, 46, 224

Tuesday, 53
tuna, 141
turquoise, 127
twenty, 66
see **regret** 64
twenty-five,
see **doughnuts**, 64
twiggy,
see **leg**, 15
twinkling,
see **eyes**, 14

U

umbrella, 205
under, 80
undergrowth, 222
understand, 172
underwater,
see **cave**, 208
unicorn,
see **scooter**, 98
uniform, 170
unique, 200
unroll, 154
unusual,
see **lamp**, 178
unwanted,
see **leftovers**, 146
unwind, 185
upset, 35, 195
upside down, 84
useless,
see **ossicone**, 14
user interface designer, 103

V

vase, 182
vertigo, 73
vibrant,
see **coral**, 208
vinegar, 141
vintage,
see **teacup**, 183
vinyl,
see **record**, 228
VR,
see **headset**, 101

W

wail, 27
wake up, 187
walk, 130
warm,
see **mittens**, 169
warning,
see **sign**, 206
wash, 160
water bottle, 133
watermelon, 151
waterproof,
see **glue**, 124
waxy,
see **crayons**, 125
wear, 94
Wednesday, 53
wetsuit, 207
wheely,
see **mid-tops**, 173
whisk, 139
white,
see **chalk**, 124
see **flour**, 141
wide-brimmed,
see **sun hat**, 168
window, 186
winged,
see **high-tops**, 173
winter, 57
wispy,
see **clouds**, 87
wobble, 197
wood-fired,
see **pizza**, 148
wooden,
see **easel**, 121
see **geta**, 170
see **spoon**, 138
wrench, 96
write, 135
writer, 106

Y

yawning, 152
yellow, 126

Z

zip line, 198

MEET THE MRS WORDSMITH TEAM

Editor-in-Chief
Sofia Fenichell

Art Director
Craig Kellman

Artists
Brett Coulson
Phillip Mamuyac
Aghnia Mardiyah
Nicolò Mereu
Daniel Permutt
Joan Varitek

Writers
Tatiana Barnes
Sawyer Eaton
Mark Holland
Amelia Mehra

Researcher
Eleni Savva

Lexicographer
Ian Brookes

Designers
Suzanne Bullat
Caroline Henriksen
Fabrice Gourdel
Holly Jones
Jess Macadam
James Sales
Lady San Pedro
Evelyn Wandernoth
James Webb

Machine Learning
Benjamin Pettit
Stanislaw Pstrokonski

Academic Advisors
Emma Madden
Prof. Susan Neuman

Producers
Eva Schumacher Payne
Leon Welters

Project Managers
Senior Editor Helen Murray
Design Manager Sunita Gahir

Senior Production Editor Jennifer Murray
US Editor Kayla Dugger
Senior Production Controller Louise Minihane
Publishing Director Mark Searle

DK Delhi
DTP Designers Satish Gaur and Rohit Rojal
Senior DTP Designer Pushpak Tyagi
Pre-production Manager Sunil Sharma
Managing Art Editor Romi Chakraborty

DK would like to thank Julia March for proofreading, Lisa Stock for editorial assistance, and Anna Formanek for design assistance.

First American Edition, 2022
Published in the United States by DK Publishing
1450 Broadway, Suite 801, New York, NY 10018

22 23 24 25 26 10 9 8 7 6 5 4 3 2
003-325948-Jan/2022

Previously published as *My Epic Life Word Book*
by Mrs Wordsmith in 2019

Published in Great Britain by Dorling Kindersley Limited

A catalog record for this book
is available from the Library of Congress.
ISBN 978-0-7440-5150-6

Printed and bound in China

For the curious
www.dk.com

mrswordsmith.com

MIX
Paper from responsible sources
FSC™ C018179
FSC www.fsc.org

This book was made with Forest Stewardship Council™ certified paper–one small step in DK's commitment to a sustainable future.

GUIDE FOR GROWN-UPS

This is not your average book. It's a book about words, but it's also a handbook for any child who wants to live a truly epic life. In this book, a cast of word-hungry animals will guide kids through everything they need to know to turn home, school, and life into a learning adventure.

This word book, illustrated by our superstar Hollywood artists, will show you that anything in life can be epic. Getting dressed in the morning? Make it epic. On your way to school? Go epic. Learning to count? Five, ten, fifteen, epic.

We designed this word book to be hilariously fun and endlessly surprising, but kids are guaranteed to learn a lot along the way. Research has proven time and again that if kids are having fun, they are in the perfect zone for deep learning. And they don't even know it!

The words in this book were curated from relevant global curriculum lists for kids aged 5 to 9. But we're Mrs Wordsmith, so we added more challenging words to the mix, like devour and reflect. We also paired everyday words with useful, funny, or interesting collocations—or word pairs—that our data engine has identified as being worth learning.

We know that even the smallest children are capable of learning big words and accelerating their vocabulary knowledge. And big kids need to learn how to read and manipulate words they already know. So there's something here for everyone. Those who aren't reading yet may need a little help from a grown-up, but confident readers can take this book to a quiet spot and get lost in it. No matter what age, we know that kids love to return to our books over and over again, whether to find the word they want or just for the fun of it.

This is a book that looks forward, not back. It gets children excited about their world today and what it might look like tomorrow, with words and illustrations focused on everything from emotions to food, hygiene to the future of technology. There will be joy. There will be tears. There will be a dog brushing his teeth on a hoverboard. Welcome to *Mrs Wordsmith Epic Words Vocabulary Book*.

"THIS IS THE WORD BOOK FOR THE 21ST CENTURY."

"This is the word book for the 21st century. I can't imagine a more delightful way to learn about words than with these wild and hilarious characters. What's especially exciting is that *Mrs Wordsmith Epic Words Vocabulary Book* uses the very latest in the science of learning to grab children's attention and teach them words about their world. Educators take note! This book will not only improve children's vocabulary, it will accelerate it at epic speed."

SUSAN NEUMAN

Professor of Childhood Education and Literacy Development, NYU

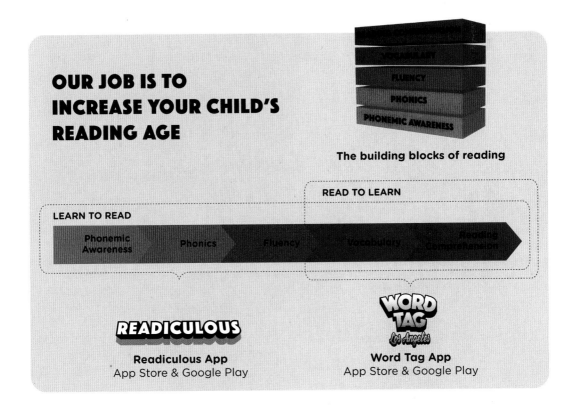

OUR JOB IS TO INCREASE YOUR CHILD'S READING AGE

VOCABULARY
FLUENCY
PHONICS
PHONEMIC AWARENESS

The building blocks of reading

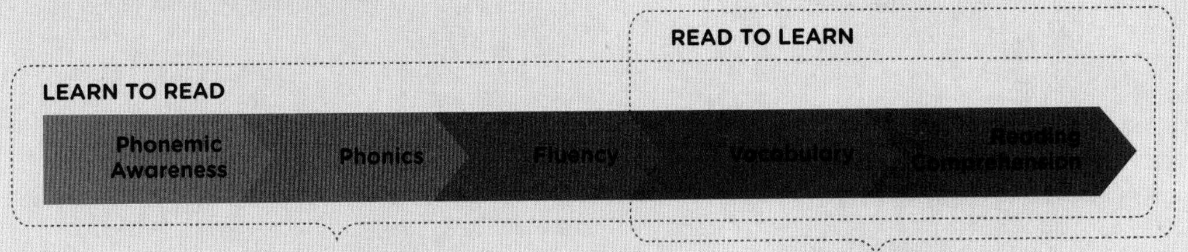
READ TO LEARN
LEARN TO READ
Phonemic Awareness
Phonics
Fluency
Vocabulary
Reading Comprehension

READICULOUS

Readiculous App
App Store & Google Play

WORD TAG Los Angeles

Word Tag App
App Store & Google Play

This book adheres to the science of reading. Our research-backed learning helps children progress through phonemic awareness, phonics, fluency, vocabulary, and reading comprehension.